PRAYER

Level <u>Dalet</u>

A Teacher's Guide

By Gail Zaiman Dorph

Edited by Barry W. Holtz

Curriculum Supervisor Seymour Fox

THE MELTON GRADED CURRICULUM SERIES

The Melton Research Center

The Jewish Theological Seminary of America

Published by the Melton Research Center
of the Jewish Theological Seminary of America
3080 Broadway, New York, New York 10027

PRINTED IN THE UNITED STATES OF AMERICA

CONTENTS

INTRODUCTION

In the alef, bet, and gimmel years of the religious school, the Melton tefillah materials have focused on:

a. the geography of the Siddur

b. the core (מַטְבֵּעַ) of the daily and Shabbat services

In the dalet year, the materials are linked to the holiday liturgy. One of the major characteristics of Jewish holidays is that each has unique liturgical elements. As each holiday approaches, students will be studying one of its unique texts and the ideas which the text expresses about the holiday.

Please note that although the tefillah curriculum was designed to be used in conjunction with the dalet level Holidays curriculum that Melton has also developed, it is possible to adapt it for use without those materials.

There are eleven lessons in this series. An outline of these lessons (which includes topic, text and key ideas) follows. Lessons are described in more detail in the Overview which introduces each lesson. Unless otherwise indicated each of these is a single lesson of approximately 45-50 minutes in length. Each lesson includes at least one tefillah text. You must decide if students will be required to learn to read the text fluently in Hebrew. If so (and we certainly encourage you to work for fluency) allow enough time in subsequent lessons for reading practice. In most lessons, students are asked to look at the Hebrew text for some information. It is not assumed that the students' Hebrew will be good enough to understand the texts without English translation.

1. ROSH HASHANAH AND YOM KIPPUR

Texts: "כִּי אָנוּ עַמֶּךָ, וְאַתָּה אֱלֹהֵינוּ" and "כִּי הִנֵּה כַּחֹמֶר בְּיַד הַיוֹצֵר"

Ideas: Rosh HaShanah and Yom Kippur are times to think about our relationship to God. In these two פִּיּוּטִים (liturgical poems) students are introduced to traditional analogies that attempt to portray the relationship between God and human beings. The lesson asks students to think about their own personal ideas and connections to God.

2. SUKKOT

Text: יַעֲלֶה וְיָבֹא

Idea: The יַעֲלֶה וְיָבֹא, which is added to the Amidah and Birkat HaMazon on Sukkot (and other holidays), reminds us of Temple times and of the sacrificial system. It links us to this core experience (the coming to the Temple with sacrifices on the three pilgrimage festivals) in the history of our people. When we recite the יַעֲלֶה וְיָבֹא, we connect ourselves to those times and that experience.

3.& 4. SHABBAT -- two lesson unit

Text: קְדֻשַּׁת הַיּוֹם: Middle berakha of the Amidah, in each of the Shabbat services

Ideas: Each of these berakhot develops the theme of the holiness of the Shabbat in a unique way. Together these texts tell a story about the Jewish people. When we recite these berakhot, we connect ourselves to this story.

5. HANUKKAH

Text: עַל הַנִּסִּים; הַנֵּרוֹת הַלָּלוּ

Idea: Students explore the concept "miracle," studying in particular Martin Buber's definition: "miracle is simply what happens; in so far as it meets people who are capable of receiving it." Students examine this definition and others and then attempt their own personal definitions of miracle.

6. TU BISHVAT

Texts: בִּרְכַּת הַשָּׁנִים

Idea: Holidays express in a unique and "once a year" way ideas that we recall each day. Tu BiShvat reminds us of two such ideas: our personal connection to אֶרֶץ יִשְׂרָאֵל and not to "take things for granted."

7.& 8. ROSH HODESH--two lesson unit to be taught before Rosh Hodesh Adar

Text: בִּרְכַּת הַחֹדֶשׁ

Idea: Rosh Hodesh links us to our past (to the time before the existence of the calendar as we know it today) and to our present (a time when the unity of the Jewish people is expressed by our use of a special calendar).

9. HALLEL (PESAH)

Texts: Selections from הַלֵּל and בִּרְכַּת גְאֻלָּה

Idea: Prayers try to recapture our peoples' emotional "highs" with words. Students compare and contrast ways in which the הַלֵּל and בִּרְכַּת גְאֻלָּה describe the experience of the Exodus from Egypt.

10. YOM HA'ATZMA'UT

Texts: Deuteronomy 16, Numbers 28 and 29, Book of Esther--chapter 9, versions of עַל הַנִּסִּים for Hanukkah, Purim, and Yom Ha'atzma'ut

Idea: What makes an event a holiday in the Jewish tradition is the Jewish people's interpretation of the event as an experience of the presence of God and the subsequent creation of liturgical expressions which mark the experience.

11. SHAVUOT

Texts: חֲתִימוֹת of middle berakhot of the Amidah and וַיְכֻלּוּ

Idea: Two possibilities for the source of קְדֻשָּׁה or holiness of our holidays are presented. The source of the קְדֻשָּׁה is God and/or the Jewish people. The goal of the lesson is to help students understand the role that each individual plays in keeping Jewish tradition, (represented here by the Jewish holidays), alive.

How to Use This Curriculum

We have tried to design this book to help facilitate its use by teachers. At the beginning of each lesson an Overview is given in which we present the goals and direction of the lesson. Following the Overview, the teaching session is divided into three parts: <u>Setting the Stage</u>, <u>Lesson</u>, <u>Closing</u>. Any worksheets or readings needed are placed after the Closing.

On the page we have tried through the graphic design to indicate the use of the curriculum. At times the curriculum addresses the teacher directly. These sections begin at the left-hand margins. In other places the curriculum indicates words addressed by the teacher to the students. Although these appear in the form of "scripts" we do not intend for them to be read to the students! These are merely examples of the kinds of explanations or discussions that we envision happening at that point. These sections are indicated by being indented from the left-hand margin. Parts of the "teacher talk" sections are in bold type and underlined. In general these are specific questions that could be used in the discussion with the students. <u>Possible</u> student answers are given in parentheses below these questions. Of course students

3

will come up with many different answers, (and some questions have no one "right" answer), but teachers have found that they are helped by seeing some possible answers that can be anticipated. A brief explanatory note to the teacher in the midst of these questions is indicated by italics:

Remarks to the teacher look like this

When the teacher speaks to the students it looks like this

(Possible student answers look like this)

Brief explanatory notes to the teacher look like this

Finally, all works of curriculum must be adapted to the specific classroom situation. Only you the teacher can know the abilities and interests and needs of your students.

Throughout this curriculum we have tried to use the English translation most appropiate for the educational purpose of each individual lesson. In addition we wanted to use these lessons as a way of helping the students gain familiarity with the book used by their congregation. Because every synagogue chooses its own particular prayerbook, we have tried to assist the teacher by giving page references in each lesson to the two most widely used Conservative prayerbooks:

"Silverman" refers to The Sabbath and Festival Prayerbook, edited by Rabbi Morris Silverman (New York: The Rabbinical Assembly, 1946).

"Siddur Sim Shalom" refers to the prayerbook edited by Rabbi Jules Harlow (New York: The Rabbinical Assembly, 1985).

Aside from these two works, on occasion we refer to the Weekday Prayer Book, edited by Rabbi Gershon Hadas (New York: The Rabbinical Assembly, 1961).

ROSH HASHANAH AND YOM KIPPUR

Overview

In this lesson, students study two פִּיּוּטִים (liturgical poems) which are part of the Yom Kippur liturgy--"כִּי הִנֵּה כַּחֹמֶר בְּיַד הַיּוֹצֵר". Text can be found in Silverman 234 and Harlow 394-5

and

"כִּי אָנוּ עַמֶּךָ, וְאַתָּה אֱלֹהֵינוּ". Text can be found in the Silverman Maḥzor on page 238-9 and in Harlow p. 400-1

These פִּיּוּטִים present us with a series of images depicting ways in which our connectedness to God has been expressed. These images stress the interdependence of human beings and God.

In this lesson, students will be introduced to these traditional images. They will analyze them and reflect on what these images teach us, by analogy, about the relationship of people and God. Students will have an opportunity to personalize this learning experience in two ways:

a) by choosing a traditional analogy that is particularly meaningful to them

b) by inventing a new analogy that they feel captures their own understanding of the relationship between humanity and the Divine.

See also Holidays for The Dalet Year, Booklet 1, p.22

Setting the Stage

Begin by saying:

> Well, here we are, back in religious school for another year. Each year we spend time talking about Rosh HaShanah and Yom Kippur. We spend such a little time, not because Rosh HaShanah and Yom Kippur are unimportant, but because of how close they come to the beginning of the school year.

> When you were younger our curriculum focused on "taking stock" as the main theme of Rosh HaShanah and Yom Kippur.

Can someone tell us what they remember about this idea of "taking stock?" What does it mean?

(It refers to thinking about ourselves and about our relationships with other people; did we treat others well or badly; are there things that we did that we are sorry for and that we would like to do differently in the coming year?)

The Hebrew word for this process of "taking stock"--referring both to thinking about our relationships with others and to doing something about it--is תְּשׁוּבָה.

Write the word תְּשׁוּבָה on the board in Hebrew.

Who can translate the word תְּשׁוּבָה?

(turning and changing, repentance)

Who remembers what is involved in doing תְּשׁוּבָה?

Last year students learned the following steps in doing teshuvah, based on Maimonides' laws of repentance in the Mishneh Torah.

-admitting to what you did wrong

-saying you're sorry

-asking forgiveness

-promising not to do it again

In what Hebrew month does the process of doing תְּשׁוּבָה begin?

(month of אֱלוּל)

So far so good. You remember well what we studied in previous years. You have a good sense of teshuvah. But...until now we have only been talking about "stock taking" and teshuvah as it relates to our relationships with other people.

There is another kind of "stock taking" associated with the High Holiday season, particularly with Yom Kippur, and that is "taking stock" of our relationship with God. That's going to be our topic in this lesson.

Lesson

Thinking about our relationship to God is difficult for most people. I know that it is for me. Yet, part of the process of doing teshuvah requires that we do think about God and our relationship to God. Usually this process is a very individual one. It takes place when we are alone. It takes place in the synagogue when we are praying.

This year, we are going to begin this special kind of "stock taking" here in class. We are going to use the Maḥzor to help us. We are going to study together two פִּיוּטִים or prayer poems that are part of the Yom Kippur service.

Write פִּיוּט *and* פִּיוּטִים *on the blackboard in Hebrew*

Both of these פִּיוּטִים use analogies to compare people and God in order to help us understand more about people and God and the relationship between us. When we invent an analogy we compare two things not ordinarily compared.

<u>For example, poets have compared love to a rose.</u>

<u>What kinds of things might they mean to say when they make this kind of comparison? How can love be like a rose?</u>

> (A rose is beautiful, love can be beautiful. A rose could smell sweet; love can be sweet smelling. A rose has thorns and can hurt you if you don't know how to handle it properly; love also needs to be handled carefully and properly.)

Based on this short exercise, we realize that we have learned something about love by comparing it to a rose. Love is not the same as a rose, but comparing love to a rose may help us understand it better.

<u>Let's do one more comparison. How can a friend be like the weather?</u>

> (One day s/he can be stormy, another day mild; one day, sunny; another day cloudy; one day, warm; another day cold.)

Again the analogy or comparison gave us a way in which we could think about our friend that was a little bit different and that added an interesting insight into who our friend is. Our friend and the weather are not the same thing, but there are ways in which our understanding of both is enriched by the analogy.

Now I think we are ready to study the two פִּיוּטִים and the analogies they use. Both use analogies to talk about God and the relationships that we have with God. Analogies are helpful to us when we try to talk about God. Usually, we don't think about ourselves as knowing much of anything about God because we can't see or touch God directly. When we use analogies to compare God to things that we do know, we help ourselves learn more about how we think and feel about God.

The first פִּיוּט we will study is recited on Yom Kippur evening as part of the same service in which we recite the כָּל נִדְרֵי. It is called "כִּי הִנֵּה כַּחֹמֶר בְּיַד הַיּוֹצֵר".

7

If you have access to <u>mahzorim</u> *with a good English translation, use them. Otherwise you may use the xeroxed copy of the* פִּיּוּט *found at the conclusion of the lesson.*

Ask for a volunteer to read the first verse in English.

<u>To what is God compared?</u>

(potter)

<u>To what are people compared?</u>

(clay)

Now I'd like you to read through the rest of the verses. As you read, find the analogies for God and the analogy for people used in each verse.

This reading can be done by the group as a whole or in small groups. If you divide the class into groups of two or three students each, allow about five minutes for students to work on the remaining verses. Give students a copy of the worksheet, which can be found at the end of the lesson, to help focus their reading.

Whether the reading is done by the class as a whole or by small groups, create a chart of the paired images on the board. The board will look like their worksheet:

כִּי הִנֵּה כַּחֹמֶר בְּיַד הַיּוֹצֵר

To what are we compared?	*To what is God compared?*
clay	potter
stone	mason
iron	blacksmith
rudder	helmsman
glass	glazier

8

Now let's examine these analogies and try to find out something about how the author of this פיוט understood the relationship of people and God.

OPTIONAL ACTIVITY: In order to help students better understand the analogy, you might give each student a piece of clay to work for a few moments before beginning the following set of questions.

<u>Let's start with clay and the potter. A potter, of course is a craftsperson who works with clay. What is the relationship of a potter and clay?</u>

(A potter works with clay, shapes it, and molds it.)

<u>How could the author of this פיוט compare the relationship of God and people to a potter and clay? What do they have in common?</u> *Allow for a variety of answers.*

(Possible answers include: Just as a potter has total control over the clay, so does God have control over people and what they become.

Some people think that God, like the potter, makes all the decisions about the clay, that is, people.)

<u>Is it only a one way relationship? Does the clay have anything to do with the relationship?</u>

(Maybe. Some clay may be better to work with than other clay.)

When students have finished exploring the images of the potter and clay and what this analogy can teach us about the relationship of God and people, ask them to work on one or two other pairs of relationships listed on the board. The purpose of this exercise is to elicit their ideas about how the relationships described by the author of the פיוט can teach us about the relationship of God and people. Students can do this work alone, in pairs or as a whole group.

You might want to ask them which of these other images they are familiar with in order to decide which pairs to work on. The questions they need to ask include:

<u>What is the relationship of _____ and _____? (e.g. clay and potter)</u>
[Use the various analogies mentioned in the poem--stone/mason, etc.]

<u>Is it a one way or two way relationship?</u>

<u>What could the author of the פיוט have had in mind about the relationship of God and people that suggested comparing their relationship to _____ and _____? (In other words, how could the author compare _____ to _____? What do they have in common?</u>

When they complete their work, you may want to ask for sharing of specific answers. Then you may ask:

<u>What do all these relationships seem to have in common?</u>

(Answers might include: God and people are connected in a complicated way. They interact with each other. God seems to stay in charge, but does not seem to have total control over people.

God has a lot of control over people.

People may influence God's activity and power.)

<u>If all these relationships and images have so much in common, why do you think the author of the פִּיוּט includes so many images? Wouldn't one or two images make the point?</u>

(Perhaps, because people are different from each other and thus need different images to help them express their thoughts and feelings about God.)

We've learned some interesting ideas from the פִּיוּט about how analogies can help us imagine God and our relationship to God. Let's examine one more פִּיוּט. It also is found in the <u>mahzor</u> in the services for Yom Kippur. It's called "כִּי אָנוּ עַמֶּךָ, וְאַתָּה אֱלֹהֵינוּ".

Again, if possible, have students find the פִּיוּט in their <u>mahzorim</u>. A copy of the פִּיוּט is found at the end of the lesson if you prefer xeroxing it.) This פִּיוּט also uses analogies to describe the relationship between God and people.

<u>Read the first two lines in Hebrew.</u>

<u>To whom are people compared? (God's עַם or people; God's children)</u>

<u>To whom is God compared? (To our father)</u>

Again, I'd like you to read through the whole פִּיוּט. *Find the analogies used to describe the relationships between God and people. This time, you'll find the relationships not in long verses, but in sentence clauses like the ones we just examined. Each clause states: we are.....; you are.....*

Again, this exercise can be done by individuals, by students working in small groups, or by the class as a whole. There is a worksheet at the end of the lesson, called "אָנוּ עַמֶּךָ, וְאַתָּה אֱלֹהֵינוּ" that can be used to focus their work.

Whether the reading is done by the class as a whole or by small groups, write the pairs of images on the board. The board will then look like their worksheet:

כִּי אָנוּ עַמֶּךָ, וְאַתָּה אֱלֹהֵינוּ

We are your...	You are our...
your people	our God
your children	our Father
your servants	our Master
your congregation	only One
your heritage	our Destiny
your flock	our Sheperd
your vineyard	our Watchman
your creatures	our Creator
your faithful	our Beloved
your treasure	our Protector
your subjects	our King

Let's examine some of these analogies more closely.

Let's start with the pair--child and father.

<u>Can a person be a father if he doesn't have any children?</u>

(no)

<u>Can a child come into the world without being fathered?</u>

(no)

<u>Why do you think the author of the פּיוּט used this relationship to describe how people and God are connected to each other?</u>

(Perhaps, just as a child needs a father to come into existence, so does a person need God in order to exist.

Perhaps, each needs the other in order to exist.

Perhaps, just as a child needs a father, so do people need God.

Perhaps, just as a father needs a child, so does God need people.)

When students seem to have finished exploring the ways in which this analogy can help us think about the relationship of people and God, explore one other pair of relationships together.

<u>Let's examine another pair. How about watchman and vineyard? What's the relationship of a watchman and a vineyard?</u>

(A watchman is responsible for taking care of the vineyard, and protecting it.

A vineyard doesn't seem to have any responsibility toward the watchman. It doesn't take care of him or owe him anything.)

<u>So far, it seems as if this analogy describes a one way relationship. Can you think of any ways in which this relationship goes both ways?</u>

(Well, I guess you can't be a watchman without something to watch. If not taken care of, the vineyard could be destroyed; so you might say that it needs the watchman in order to exist.)

<u>Why do you think the author of this פּיוּט used this analogy to describe the connection between people and God? What can we learn from this comparison?</u>

(Perhaps, the relationship of God to people is a relationship of a caretaker to something that needs taking care of. Perhaps, people's relationship to

God involves being taken care of. Perhaps, people need to be taken care of in order to exist, and God serves as the Caretaker or Watchman.)

At this point, ask students to work on one or two other pairs of relationships listed on the board. Again, the purpose of the exercise is to elicit their ideas about how the relationships described by the author of the פִּיּוּט can teach us about the relationships of God and people. Students may work in groups of two's or three's or individually.

The questions they need to be asking as they work include:

(Again insert phrases of the analogies we have been working with in the blank spaces:)

What is the relationship of _____ and _____ ?

Is it a one way or two way relationship?

What could the author of the פִּיּוּט have wanted to teach us about the relationship of God and people that suggested comparing their relationship to _____ and _____ ?

When they have completed their work, you may want to ask for some sharing of specific answers. Then ask:

What, if anything, do all these relationships have in common?

(Answers might include:

They seem to imply some kind of interdependence.

The relationships all seem to go both ways.

Even though God seems to need people, God seems the more powerful party in all the relationships.

Without people, God wouldn't be much, because all these relationships seem to imply that God, although more powerful than people, could not exist outside of a relationship with people.)

Again, you might ask:

Why do you think so many images are used in the פִּיּוּט to describe the relationship of God and people?

(The answer would obviously reflect the same notion, that is, that people are different and so different analogies, different images would be meaningful to different people.)

Studying these two פִּיּוּטִים has given us interesting insights into the nature of the relationship of people and God. You may want to study these relationships more closely when you are in the synagogue on Yom Kippur. You may want to discuss these relationships with your families.

Closing

Let's finish today by doing some writing as a way of reflecting and summarizing our discussion. I'm going to ask you to answer two questions on separate 3 x 5 cards. We'll put the answers into two different baskets (or whatever kind of container you choose). Then we'll share our answers through "secret sharing."

"Secret sharing" is a technique for sharing anonymously information that may be considered personal. In this case, students will write their answers, but not their names, on 3 x 5 cards and put the cards in a container. Students will then pick a card out of the basket and read the answer that appears on the card. Thus answers will be shared anonymously.

You may want to write the following two questions on the board in addition to saying them aloud.

First, look back over both of these פֵּירוּטִים. After rereading them, choose the analogy that best describes your idea--for right now--of the relationship between people and God. When you've decided on your favorite, write it on a 3 x 5 card. Include one sentence which explains your choice. The sentence could begin with, "I chose the relationship _____ and_____ because..."

Second, if you were going to invent a new image for the relationship between God and people, what would it be? The sentence could begin with, "If I were to invent a new image for the relationship between God and people it would be_____ and _____because..."

When students have finished writing, ask them to put each response into a separate basket or container. Mix up the response within each basket. Pass the baskets and ask every student to take one 3 x 5 card out of each basket. Go around the room, allowing time for students to read the answers on their cards.

When they have completed the reading, you may ask for additional comments. You might wrap up the lesson by reminding students to pay special attention to these פֵּירוּטִים at their Yom Kippur service and by asking students to ask the members of their families to also think about the relationship between God and people and invent a new image to express that relationship.

"כִּי הִנֵּה כַחֹמֶר בְּיַד הַיּוֹצֵר"

WORKSHEET

Part I

To what are we compared?   To what is God compared?

_____   _____

_____   _____

_____   _____

_____   _____

_____   _____

_____   _____

"כִּי אָנוּ עַמֶּךָ, וְאַתָּה אֱלֹקֵינוּ"

WORKSHEET

Part II

Your are Our...   We are your...

_____

_____

_____

_____

_____

_____

כִּי אָנוּ עַמֶּךְ וְאַתָּה אֱלֹהֵינוּ . אָנוּ בָנֶיךָ וְאַתָּה אָבִינוּ
אָנוּ עֲבָדֶיךָ וְאַתָּה אֲדוֹנֵנוּ . אָנוּ קְהָלֶךָ וְאַתָּה חֶלְקֵנוּ
אָנוּ נַחֲלָתֶךָ וְאַתָּה גוֹרָלֵנוּ . אָנוּ צֹאנֶךָ וְאַתָּה רוֹעֵנוּ
אָנוּ כַרְמֶךָ וְאַתָּה נוֹטְרֵנוּ . אָנוּ פְעֻלָּתֶךָ וְאַתָּה יוֹצְרֵנוּ
אָנוּ רַעֲיָתֶךָ וְאַתָּה דוֹדֵנוּ . אָנוּ סְגֻלָּתֶךָ וְאַתָּה קְרוֹבֵנוּ
אָנוּ עַמֶּךָ וְאַתָּה מַלְכֵּנוּ . אָנוּ מַאֲמִירֶךָ וְאַתָּה מַאֲמִירֵנוּ

For we are Thy people, and Thou art our God;

We are Thy children, and Thou our Father.

We are Thy servants, and Thou our Master;

We are Thy congregation, and Thou our Portion.

We are Thine inheritance and Thou our Lot;

We are Thy flock, and Thou our Shepherd.

We are Thy vineyard, and Thou our Keeper;

We are Thy work, and Thou our Creator.

We are Thy faithful, and Thou our Beloved;

We are Thy loyal ones, and Thou our Lord.

We are Thy subjects, and Thou our King.

We are Thy devoted people, and Thou our exalted God.

As clay are we, as soft and yielding clay
That lies between the fingers of the potter.
At his will he moulds it thick or thin,
And forms its shape according to his fancy.
So are we in Thy hand, God of love;
 Thy covenant recall and show Thy mercy.

As stone are we, inert, resistless stone
That lies within the fingers of the mason.
At his will he keeps it firm and whole,
Or at his pleasure hews it into fragments.
So are we in Thy hand, God of life;
 Thy covenant recall and show Thy mercy.

As iron are we, as cold and rigid iron
That lies within the fingers of the craftsman.
At his will he forges it to shape,
Or draws it boldly forth to lie unbended.
So are we in Thy hand, God who saves;
 Thy covenant recall and show Thy mercy.

As glass are we, as thin, transparent glass
That lies within the fingers of the blower.
At his will, he blows it crystal clear,
Or melts it down to suit his whim or notion.
So are we in Thy hand, gracious God;
 Thy covenant recall and show Thy mercy.

As cloth are we, as formless, graceless cloth
That lies within the fingers of the draper.
At his will he shapes its lines and folds,
Or leaves it unadorned to hang unseemly.
So are we in Thy hand, righteous God;
 Thy covenant recall and show Thy mercy.

As silver are we, with metal dross alloyed
That lies within the fingers of the smelter.
At his will he fuses or refines,
Retains the slag or keeps it pure and precious.
So are we in Thy hand, healing God;
 Thy covenant recall and show Thy mercy.

Text and translation from <u>The Sabbath and Festival Prayerbook,</u> edited by Rabbi
Morris Silverman (New York: The Rabbinical Assembly, 1946).

כִּי הִנֵּה כַּחֹמֶר בְּיַד הַיּוֹצֵר. בִּרְצוֹתוֹ מַרְחִיב וּבִרְצוֹתוֹ
מְקַצֵּר. כֵּן אֲנַחְנוּ בְּיָדְךָ חֶסֶד נוֹצֵר.
לַבְּרִית הַבֵּט וְאַל תֵּפֶן לַיֵּצֶר:

כִּי הִנֵּה כָּאֶבֶן בְּיַד הַמְסַתֵּת. בִּרְצוֹתוֹ אוֹחֵז וּבִרְצוֹתוֹ
מְכַתֵּת. כֵּן אֲנַחְנוּ בְּיָדְךָ מְחַיֶּה וּמְמוֹתֵת.
לַבְּרִית הַבֵּט וְאַל תֵּפֶן לַיֵּצֶר:

כִּי הִנֵּה כַּגַּרְזֶן בְּיַד הֶחָרָשׁ. בִּרְצוֹתוֹ דִּבֶּק לָאוּר וּבִרְצוֹתוֹ
פֵּרַשׁ. כֵּן אֲנַחְנוּ בְּיָדְךָ תּוֹמֵךְ עָנִי וָרָשׁ.
לַבְּרִית הַבֵּט וְאַל תֵּפֶן לַיֵּצֶר:

כִּי הִנֵּה כַּהֶגֶה בְּיַד הַמַּלָּח. בִּרְצוֹתוֹ אוֹחֵז וּבִרְצוֹתוֹ
שִׁלַּח. כֵּן אֲנַחְנוּ בְּיָדְךָ אֵל טוֹב וְסַלָּח.
לַבְּרִית הַבֵּט וְאַל תֵּפֶן לַיֵּצֶר:

כִּי הִנֵּה כַּזְּכוּכִית בְּיַד הַמְזַגֵּג. בִּרְצוֹתוֹ חוֹגֵג. וּבִרְצוֹתוֹ
מְמוֹגֵג. כֵּן אֲנַחְנוּ בְּיָדְךָ מַעֲבִיר זָדוֹן וְשׁוֹגֵג.
לַבְּרִית הַבֵּט וְאַל תֵּפֶן לַיֵּצֶר:

כִּי הִנֵּה כַּיְרִיעָה בְּיַד הָרוֹקֵם. בִּרְצוֹתוֹ מְיַשֵּׁר וּבִרְצוֹתוֹ
מְעַקֵּם. כֵּן אֲנַחְנוּ בְּיָדְךָ אֵל קַנּוֹא וְנוֹקֵם.
לַבְּרִית הַבֵּט וְאַל תֵּפֶן לַיֵּצֶר:

כִּי הִנֵּה כַּכֶּסֶף בְּיַד הַצּוֹרֵף. בִּרְצוֹתוֹ מְסַגְסֵג וּבִרְצוֹתוֹ
מְצָרֵף. כֵּן אֲנַחְנוּ בְּיָדְךָ מַמְצִיא לְמָזוֹר תֶּרֶף.
לַבְּרִית הַבֵּט וְאַל תֵּפֶן לַיֵּצֶר:

כִּי הִנֵּה כַּחֹמֶר בְּיַד הַיֹּצֵר. בִּרְצוֹתוֹ מַרְחִיב וּבִרְצוֹתוֹ
מְקַצֵּר. כֵּן אֲנַחְנוּ בְּיָדְךָ חֶסֶד נֹצֵר.
לַבְּרִית הַבֵּט וְאַל תֵּפֶן לַיֵּצֶר:

Text and translation from The Sabbath and Festival Prayerbook, edited by Rabbi
Morris Silverman (New York: The Rabbinical Assembly, 1946).

APPENDIX

(For the Teacher)

כִּי הִנֵּה כַחֹמֶר״״

Like the clay in the hand of the potter
So are we in Thy hand

An alphabetical acrostic of unknown origin, only portions of which are included in the various recensions of the Prayer Book, the basic idea of this prayer is inspired by these verses in the Book of Jeremiah:

The word which came to Jeremiah from the Lord, saying: "Arise, and go down to the potter's house, and there I will cause thee to hear My words." Then I went down to the potter's house, and, behold he was at his work on the wheels. And whensoever the vessel that he made of the clay was marred in the hand of the potter, he made it again another vessel, as seemed good to the potter to make it.

Then the word of the Lord came to me, saying: "O house of Israel, cannot I do with you as this potter? saith the Lord. Behold, as the clay in the potter's hand, so are ye in My hand, O house of Israel. And at one instant I may speak concerning a nation, and concerning a kingdom, to pick up and to break down and to destroy it; but if that nation turn from their evil, because of which I have spoken against it, I repent of the evil that I thought to do unto it. And at one instant I may speak concerning a nation, and concerning a kingdom, to build and to plant it; but if it do evil in My sight, that it hearken not to My voice, then I repent of the good, wherewith I said I would benefit it." (Jeremiah 18:1-11)

In his parable of the potter and the clay, Jeremiah boldly declares that though man is but potter's clay in the hands of God, he nevertheless retains his freedom of choice between obedience to God's will and defiance of it. Jeremiah thus implies that God's decision is subject to man's revision, for man's repentance can reverse "an evil decree."

20

In this acrostic our poet enlarges on the same theme as he refers to various types of craftsmen: the mason, the blacksmith, the mariner, the glass blower, the embroiderer, and the silversmith. As each of them fashions his raw material, he rejects that which does not conform with his will and design. As the "raw material" in God's hands, we pray that we may be willing to be molded in accordance with His will. Man is not a pliant and responsive matter in God's hands. He may choose to resist his Maker, or yield to Him. If man shatters or breaks, if the stuff of his nature withers to the touch of God, he may be rejected. If he is firm and without incorrigible blemish, God may shape him to His will.

Comments on the text

The unknown author of this piyyut rhymed the three strophes of each stanza. Thus in the first stanza, hayotzer rhymes with mekatzer and with notzer; in the second stanza, mesattet rhymes with mekhatet and again with memotet.

The author addresses God respectively as: The Keeper of steadfast kindness, the Decreer of life and death, the Sustainer of the poor, God good and forgiving, the Pardoner of all sin, the Champion of justice, and the Healer of the ailing.

"Regard the covenant"

Each stanza culminates in the refrain: "Regard the covenant and not our corruption."

The "covenant" here refers to a phrase in Exodus 34:10: "Behold, I make a covenant." Rabbi Judah interprets this as referring to two earlier verses in which God's Thirteen Attributes would be invoked in a prayer for forgiveness, such a prayer would not be rejected(R.H. 17b)

כִּי אָנוּ עַמֶּךָ

We are Thy people and Thou art our God

We are Thy children and Thou art our Father

We are Thy faithful and Thou art our Beloved

We are insolent, but Thou art mericiful

These expressions of intimacy betweeen Israel and God are culled from various parts of the Bible. The epithets of endearment reach their climax in a declaration of mutual fealty "We are pledged to Thee and Thou art pledged to us," based on the verse

"Thou hast avouched [affirmed] the Lord this day to be thy God...And the Lord hath avouched [affirmed] thee this day to be His own treasure"(Deut. 26:17-18).

At this point there is a sharp change from a tone of confidence and elation to one of abject contrition. The contrast is now drawn between man's insolence and God's graciousness, between man's obstinacy and God's forbearance, and between man's ephemeral life and God's eternity. Nevertheless, we venture to make entreaty to God because, despite our sinfulness, there is a redeeming quality to our life, in that we confess our sins. "For we are neither so arrogant nor so hardened as to say before Thee,...'We are righteous and have not sinned.'"

From Justice and Mercy by Max Arzt (Holt, Rinehart and Winston, 1963), pp. 212-215.

SUKKOT

OVERVIEW

In this lesson, students will study the יַעֲלֶה וְיָבֹא, a text added to the Amidah and Birkat Hamazon on Sukkot and other holidays. The goal of this lesson is to expand students' knowledge and understanding of Sukkot in particular and other Jewish holidays in general. Learning about the history of the Jewish people means learning about some of the core experiences that have made Judaism what it is today. The ancient Temple service is one such core experience.

We all know that in modern times, we celebrate the holiday of Sukkot by building a sukkah and by waving the lulav and etrog. In ancient times, a third element was also a critical part of the celebration. That third element was a pilgrimage to the Temple—עֲלִיָּה לְרֶגֶל. Learning a little about the Temple experience and how it is incorporated in the holiday liturgy will be the focus of this lesson.

In the alef through gimmel years, students already have studied the historical (desert) and agricultural (early Israelite settlement in the land of Israel) sources of the holiday of Sukkot. They have learned about building a sukkah and "bensching" (saying the blessing for) lulav and etrog. In the dalet year, we will be focusing on the experience of Sukkot in the Temple. The ancient Temple service is a core experience in the history of the Jewish people. Learning about the history of the Jewish people means learning about some of the core experiences that have made Judaism what it is today.

In the Talmud (Shabbat 24a) the text, יַעֲלֶה וְיָבֹא, is referred to as מֵעֵין הַמְּאֹרָע, that is a "synopsis of the event." The Talmud uses this same term, מֵעֵין הַמְּאֹרָע, to refer to the עַל הַנִּסִּים passages inserted in the Amidah and Birkat Hamazon on Hanukkah and Purim. In both those cases it is clear that the event referred to is the event upon which the holiday itself is based. The historical event presented in the text of the יַעֲלֶה וְיָבֹא seems to be the Temple service itself. The יַעֲלֶה וְיָבֹא can be read as a description of the way in which our ancestors approached the Temple mount to bring their sacrificial offerings. During Sukkot the יַעֲלֶה וְיָבֹא prayer is added to the Birkat HaYom berakhah of the Amidah; during the intermediary days of the festival (Hol HaMoed), it is placed in the Birkat Avodah.

יַעֲלֶה, וְיָבֹא, וְיַגִּיעַ, וְיֵרָאֶה

This is the list of verbs with which the text begins: Ascend, come forward, draw near, appear. Coming to the Temple with one's holiday sacrifices was not a casual event. It was filled with ceremony and ritual. One did not just arrive, sacrifice in hand at the base of the altar. The ceremony began at the foot of the steps leading up to the Temple and continued until the worshipper reached the altar. Perhaps, by reading the text of this tefilla as a verbal reenactment of the careful way in which each Israelite approached the altar, we can gain a sense of the importance of the Temple to our ancestors. (for more information, see Donin, To Pray As A Jew, Basic Books, 1980, pp.130-132)

MATERIALS:

[Before class, prepare a chart that looks like this:]

And let this act be remembered -- וְיִזָּכֵר

Let the gift be recorded -- וְיִפָּקֵד

Let him be heard (to make his declarations) -- וְיִשָּׁמַע

Let the gift be accepted -- וְיֵרָצֶה

Appear (before the officiating kohen) -- וְיֵרָאֶה

Draw near (to the altar) -- וְיַגִּיעַ

Come forward -- וְיָבֹא

Ascend the steps -- יַעֲלֶה

SETTING THE STAGE

Have any of you ever been to a graduation or a wedding? or even seen one on T.V.? Tell me about it. How does it begin?

(marching, music, flowers,)

Why do you think that each of these ceremonies has such an elaborate and kind of stages beginning?

(open-ended question)

Can you think of other events that have elaboratye opening ceremonies?

What about the opening of a baseball game?

24

These beginning ceremonies create a certain excitement about an event. They mark each event as a separate entity. The beginning of a graduation is different from the beginning of a wedding and different from the beginning of a baseball game.

In the synagogue, we have one event that I can think of that has its own special ceremonial opening.

Can you think of what that might be?

> (Taking the Torah from the ark. Depending on the congregation the בַּר or בַּת מִצְוָה being called up to the Torah might also constitute a separate event with its own movements, music, rules.)

During Temple times, an elaborate opening ceremony also existed. It marked the special way in which each person bringing a sacrifice would come into the Temple and up to the altar to bring the offering.

In the Gimmel curriculum students studied the berakhah called Avodah which begins with the word רְצֵה. That lesson included a guided fantasy, a piece of which follows. If students did indeed study this text last year you might want to introduce it now by saying something like what follows in the brackets. Otherwise continue with the paragraph after the brackets:

[In גּ כִּתָּה, we studied a berakhah in the Amidah that reminded us of the Temple service. That Berakhah is called Avodah and began with the word רְצֵה. I'm going to reread a part of it today to set the stage for our lesson about Sukkot.]

In order to really picture what it must have been like, I'm going to ask you to close your eyes and try to picture this event.

Find a place to sit comfortably and privately. Relax. Close your eyes and breathe deeply. Try to put all thoughts out of your mind. Breathe deeply, in and out.

You're about to begin a journey: a journey of the mind. You are going to go back in your imagination over 2,000 years ago - to a time when King Solomon's Temple stood. Relax and breathe.

Imagine yourself as a farmer in the land of Israel over 2,000 years ago. It is a time when oxen or donkeys plow the land, a time when people travel by foot or on the backs of animals, a time when most people live in houses of stone or in huts of mud and straw. The skies are blue and clear. All around you are hills and fields, stones and plants, browns and greens. You can feel and smell the brisk air and the scent of freshly harvested fields.

Suddenly you find yourself in the midst of a group of people. People of all ages travelling together! Most are walking, some travel in wagons or on animals. Everyone is excited. People are laughing and talking. In the distance you can hear a group singing.

It is the end of a successful harvest season, and you are going with thousands of other Jews to Jerusalem to give thanks to God. In Jerusalem you will enter into God's Holy place, the Temple, to give your gift. You may have brought with you a goat or a ram to sacrifice upon the main altar. You have grapes, apples and oranges.

As you arrive at the top of the final hill, the breathtaking view of the Temple greets you. It is grand and bright, of gleaming limestones and gold. A tall rectangular building surrounded by space and walls.

You enter the Courtyard. On your left you see the main altar made of stone, where the animals that you brought will be sacrificed to God. An animal has recently been sacrificed by a כֹּהֵן. Its body lies on the altar, a blazing fire underneath it. Approaching the altar you can feel the heat of the fire and smell the smoke that is rising to Heaven. You watch as the animal is allowed to burn up completely. When the sacrifice is completed, the Kohanim will take the fruit and grain which you brought to their storehouses; later they will eat it.

(A Guided Tour Through The Temple by Jeff Perry-Marx for MUSE project of Hebrew Union College Skirball Museum)

LESSON

O.K., now we're ready to study a special paragraph added to the Amidah and the Birkat Hamazon on Sukkot.

I am going to read the first words of this tefilla to you. I want you to imagine where in the guided fantasy you could insert the words of the tefilla. Ready?

ASCEND THE STEPS. COME FORWARD. DRAW NEAR TO THE ALTAR. APPEAR. LET THE GIFT BE ACCEPTED. LET HIM BE HEARD. LET THE GIFT BE RECORDED. LET THIS ACT BE REMEMBERED BY GOD.

At this point, hand out copies of the guided fantasy. Reread the opening words of the יַעֲלֶה וְיָבֹא again. Ask students to find the place where the words that you have just read would fit in best.

As students reread the fantasy, they should realize that these words would best fit toward the end of their reading, at the point that the worshipper has reached the final hill and is about to enter the Temple area itself.

At this point, set up the chart that appears at the beginning of the lesson. (If impossible to prepare ahead of time, create the chart on the board while students are reading the guided fantasy to themselves.)

> <u>Before we even begin to analyze this chart, look at it carefully. What does it look like?</u>

>> (a hill, a stairway going up)

> <u>What words are on the chart?</u>

>> (The words that the teacher just read aloud.)

> <u>Let's read the words in Hebrew and English.</u> *(Perhaps, choose a different volunteer for each pair of words.)*

After reading the text through once or twice for fluency, you might say something like:

> One way to understand the opening words of the יַעֲלֶה וְיָבֹא is to picture a festival in ancient times. Our ancestors coming from all over Israel. Finally, after a long journey, they reach Jerusalem and the mountain on which the Temple stood. They ascend the mountain, coming closer and closer to the entrance of the Temple, walking up the steps, entering the courtyard, and bringing their sacrifice near enough to the altar finally to be offered to God.

At this point, you might ask for two volunteers, one to read the Hebrew and another to read the English. And two more volunteers to act out the actions that are being read. This enactment might help students understand how the text can be read as if it were meant to be a reenactment of an actual event. Once the words have been acted out, you might say something like:

> Had we lived in ancient Israel, these words might have been said to each and everyone of us as we prepared to bring our offering. Let's continue in our reading of the text.

At this point, ask students to open their siddurim to the יַעֲלֶה וְיָבֹא text. A copy of an English and Hebrew text can be found at the end of this lesson, but it is always preferable to use the siddur that the congregation itself uses if it has an adequate English translation. סִדּוּר שִׂים שָׁלוֹם does not have a literal translation of this text, so we are including a translation that appears in the <u>Rabbinical Assembly Daily Prayer Book</u> at the end of this lesson.

> <u>Begin to read the text in Hebrew, when you find the words יַעֲלֶה וְיָבֹא, raise your hand.</u>

O.K., now you've found the name of the tefilla and the beginning of the chain of words that we've been studying. The opening words of this tefilla try to capture the drama, the pageantry of what it was like to bring a sacrifice to the Temple in ancient times. If you continue to read the words of the text however, you will find no mention of sacrifices.

<u>What word follows the words that appear on our chart?</u>

(remembrances)

Today we no longer bring sacrifices to the Temple, not even if we live in Israel. Instead we bring instead remembrances, recollections, memories. Let's read on to try and understand what that means....to bring remembrances.

<u>What kind of remembrances are mentioned?</u>

(remembrances of our ancestors, remembrances of the Messiah, remembrances of Jerusalem, remembrances of all the people, the House of Israel)

<u>What kinds of remembrances or memories are these?</u>

(They are memories about our people's past.)

<u>How do you think we actually can bring remembrances?</u>

(open-ended questions)

<u>That's a tough question. Think for a minute about your own family.</u>

<u>Do you have any special family stories, special family memories? What makes those particular moments special?</u>

(Allow for a variety of answers)

<u>How do you remember these events?</u>

(We talk about them; we show pictures of them.)

Talking and taking pictures is a lot like what the text means when it says we bring remembrances. The יַעֲלֶה וְיָבֹא is a little like our Jewish family scrapbook or our Jewish history story that we tell each other. It's like saying: once upon a time a long time ago, the Jewish people lived all together in the land of Israel. Three times a year, we came together to celebrate holidays at the Temple in Jerusalem And what a celebration that was! Everyone was there. It was beautiful; it was fun; it was exciting. We brought sacrifices to God; we feasted; it was fantastic!

<u>So when we recite the יַעֲלֶה וְיָבֹא, in what way are we bringing remembrances?</u>

(We're talking about the past.)

When the יַעֲלֶה וְיָבֹא was written, there was already no Temple and people no longer brought sacrifices. Prayer, particularly the Amidah, took the place of sacrifices. When we recite the יַעֲלֶה וְיָבֹא it as though we are bringing the remembrances of our Jewish past before God in much the same way that our ancestors brought their sacrifices. When our ancestors brought their sacrifices, it was almost as though they were bringing God a gift---and they hoped that God in turn would give them gifts.

<u>Look at the last few lines of the tefilla. What kinds of gifts do we ask God for?</u>

(Remember us for good, for blessing, for life)

Closing

You might use the following two questions to conclude the lesson. You could ask students to write the answer to each question before they share, or you could have them share sentence whip style reminding students that they always have the option to pass.

<u>If you were going to add your own remembrances to the יַעֲלֶה וְיָבֹא, what would you include?</u>

<u>If you were going to add to the list of blessings or gifts that we would want from God, what would you add to the final list in the tefilla?</u>

TEXT FOR STUDENTS

On Rosh Ḥodesh and Ḥol Hamoʻed

Our God and God of our fathers, on this day of

Rosh Ḥodesh   Pesaḥ   Sukkot

Remember our fathers and be gracious to us;
Consider all Israel standing before You in prayer
For the Messianic era of deliverance
And for Jerusalem, Your holy city.

Mercifully grant us life, deliverance, and peace.
Bless us, O Lord our God, with all that is good.

Remember Your promise of mercy and redemption;
Be merciful to us and save us.
It is to You that we lift our eyes.
Gracious and compassionate are You, O our King.

From the Weekday Prayer Book, edited by Rabbi Gershon Hadas (New York: The Rabbinical Assembly, 1961).

TEXT FOR STUDENTS

לראש חודש ולחול המועד

אֱלֹהֵינוּ וֵאלֹהֵי אֲבוֹתֵינוּ,

יַעֲלֶה וְיָבֹא, וְיַגִּיעַ וְיֵרָאֶה, וְיֵרָצֶה וְיִשָּׁמַע,

וְיִפָּקֵד וְיִזָּכֵר זִכְרוֹנֵנוּ וּפִקְדוֹנֵנוּ, וְזִכְרוֹן אֲבוֹתֵינוּ,

וְזִכְרוֹן מָשִׁיחַ בֶּן־דָּוִד עַבְדֶּךָ, וְזִכְרוֹן יְרוּשָׁלַיִם עִיר קָדְשֶׁךָ,

וְזִכְרוֹן כָּל־עַמְּךָ בֵּית יִשְׂרָאֵל לְפָנֶיךָ, לִפְלֵיטָה וּלְטוֹבָה,

לְחֵן וּלְחֶסֶד וּלְרַחֲמִים, לְחַיִּים וּלְשָׁלוֹם, בְּיוֹם

חַג הַסֻּכּוֹת הַזֶּה   חַג הַמַּצּוֹת הַזֶּה   רֹאשׁ הַחֹדֶשׁ הַזֶּה

זָכְרֵנוּ, יְיָ אֱלֹהֵינוּ, בּוֹ לְטוֹבָה,

וּפָקְדֵנוּ בוֹ לִבְרָכָה, וְהוֹשִׁיעֵנוּ בוֹ לְחַיִּים,

וּבִדְבַר יְשׁוּעָה וְרַחֲמִים חוּס וְחָנֵּנוּ, וְרַחֵם עָלֵינוּ וְהוֹשִׁיעֵנוּ,

כִּי אֵלֶיךָ עֵינֵינוּ, כִּי אֵל מֶלֶךְ חַנּוּן וְרַחוּם אָתָּה.

From the Weekday Prayer Book, edited by Rabbi Gershon Hadas (New York: The Rabbinical Assembly, 1961).

SHABBAT--Two Lessons

Overview

In this two lesson unit, students will study the Shabbat Amidah. The Shabbat Amidah differs from the weekly Amidah in two ways. On Shabbat, the Amidah has only one middle berakha. It is referred to as קְדֻשַׁת הַיּוֹם. Its content teaches us about the sanctity of Shabbat. On weekdays, in the middle section there are thirteen berakhot of בַּקָשָׁה, request. In addition, at all daily services the middle section of the Amidah is the same. On Shabbat, the middle berakha is different in each service. Although in each service the theme of the berakha is קְדֻשַׁת הַיּוֹם, the holiness of the Shabbat, this holiness is expressed differently each time we pray. The theme of the middle berakha of the Amidah of Erev Shabbat is the connection of Shabbat to the creation of the world. In the Amidah for Shaharit, Shabbat is described in terms of its connection to the revelation at Sinai. In the Amidah of Musaf, Shabbat is described in terms of its connection to the Temple service. In the Amidah of Minha, Shabbat is described in terms of its connection to the messianic era. Thus, each of these berakhot develops the theme of the sanctity of Shabbat in a unique way. Through their thematic content, these texts tell a story about the Jewish people. When we recite these berakhot, we connect ourselves to this story.

It is the purpose of these two lessons to introduce students to each of these berakhot and its theme. In the first lesson, students will review information about the Amidah in general and the Shabbat Amidah in particular. They will study the one paragraph of the קְדֻשַׁת הַיּוֹם section that appears in every service, the paragraph that begins אֱלֹהֵינוּ וֵאלֹהֵי אֲבוֹתֵינוּ, רְצֵה בִמְנוּחָתֵנוּ. In lesson two, they will examine the remainder of the section known as קְדֻשַׁת הַיּוֹם for each service. The chart at the end of lesson two will help them keep track of the differences between these berakhot. The unit ends with a synthesis activity. Students are asked to create a mural which graphically portrays the themes of these berakhot. The mural will include a separate section for each berakha.

33

Lesson One

Setting the Stage

Begin by saying something along the following lines:

Each year that we have been in religious school, we have learned about Shabbat. That's because the Shabbat is so important to the Jewish people. If someone were going to ask you what is the most important thing you've learned about Shabbat in religious school, what would you say? (open-ended)

This year we will again spend some time thinking and studying about Shabbat. Just as we have studied Siddur texts to learn more about Rosh HaShanah, Yom Kippur, and Sukkot, we will examine several Siddur texts in order to learn more about Shabbat. We're going to do this by carefully studying each Amidah that we recite on Shabbat.

Lesson

Let's begin our study with a mini-review.

First of all--during which weekday services do we recite the Amidah?

(מַעֲרִיב sometimes called ,עַרְבִית, מִנְחָה, שַׁחֲרִית)

As students answer, list the names of the daily services on the board in Hebrew.

Great. That's correct. We recite the Amidah at each and every daily service. That is true on Shabbat also. Except that on Shabbat, we recite the Amidah four times, not three times. The reason for this is the additional--מוּסָף service. מוּסָף, meaning "added", follows the Shaharit service on Shabbat morning.

Now let's create a list of the Shabbat services at which we recite the Amidah.

As students list the names of the services, list them on the board in Hebrew. Chart should look like this:

Daily services - חוֹל   Shabbat services - שַׁבָּת

עַרְבִית   עַרְבִית

(Continues on next page)

34

שַׁחֲרִית   שַׁחֲרִית

                                              מוּסָף

מִנְחָה   מִנְחָה

<u>Look at the two listings on the board. How are they different from each other?</u>

Each weekday, there are three services: עַרְבִית ,מִנְחָה ,שַׁחֲרִית. Shabbat has four or four and a half services. It starts with קַבָּלַת שַׁבָּת before עַרְבִית on Friday night and the next day continues with שַׁחֲרִית, מוּסָף, מִנְחָה, עַרְבִית לְמוֹצָאֵי שַׁבָּת.

Add קַבָּלַת שַׁבָּת before עַרְבִית to chart in Shabbat column.

<u>Now that we've talked about the services themselves, let's focus on the Amidah of these services which is the focus of our lesson. How many berakhot does the weekday Amidah have?</u>

      (19)

<u>Who remembers how many berakhot the Shabbat Amidah contains?</u>

      (7)

On Shabbat, the Amidah has only 7 berakhot. The first 3 and the last 3 are exactly the same as the weekday berakhot.

<u>Let's take a minute to review the names of these berakhot.</u>

Take a minute to ask students for names of each of the first and last berakhot. They are:

Berakha #1 = אָבוֹת

Berakha #2 = גְבוּרוֹת

Berakha #3 = קְדֻשַׁת הַשֵּׁם

Third from the end = עֲבוֹדָה

Second from the end = הוֹדָאָה

Last = בִּרְכַּת הַשָּׁלוֹם

On Shabbat, there is only one middle berakha. It is called קְדֻשַׁת הַיוֹם.

Write the words קְדֻשַׁת הַיוֹם *on the blackboard in Hebrew.*

35

This berakha is called קְדֻשַּׁת הַיּוֹם, and although the berakha always has the same חֲתִימָה, the words in the paragraphs before the חֲתִימָה are different in each service.

Write the חֲתִימָה *on the board in Hebrew:* בָּרוּךְ אַתָּה ה׳ מְקַדֵּשׁ הַשַּׁבָּת

This year we're going to study each of these middle berakhot carefully in order to learn what each can teach us about Shabbat.

Before we actually examine the texts of these berakhot, I'd like you to take out a piece of paper and make a list of ideas and themes that you might include if you were creating a berakha designed to be recited specifically on Shabbat.

You can ask students to do this assignment individually or in small groups. When they have worked for about five minutes, regroup and list their answers on the board.

Answers might include themes such as rest or not working, setting aside a special time different from the other days of the week, etc.

Now that we've thought about the question from our own points of view, let's find out how the Siddur answers this very question. We're going to start by reading the one paragraph that is included in each version of the berakha, קְדֻשַּׁת הַיּוֹם. It is the paragraph that includes the חֲתִימָה. You'll find it on pages 298-299 of <u>Siddur Sim Shalom</u> (ed. Jules Harlow) and on page 22 of the Silverman <u>Sabbath and Festival Prayer Book</u>. The paragraph begins with the words, אֱלֹהֵינוּ וֵאלֹהֵי אֲבוֹתֵינוּ.

Read the paragraph aloud in Hebrew. Point out the חֲתִימָה.

Now read the paragraph in English. It's not an easy paragraph to understand. Try to figure out what it actually says about Shabbat. *Ask for student response.*

Response should include something like:

Israel has inherited the Shabbat, we add holiness to our lives through the mitzvot, it's important to rest on Shabbat

<u>Based on your reading of it, does it seem as though there are any themes or ideas included in it that are the same as the ideas that we've listed on the board? What are they?</u>

(maybe something about resting, maybe something about the specialness of the Shabbat)

<u>Are there ideas or themes listed that are different from those that we've already mentioned?</u>

(the notion of inheriting the Shabbat)

36

In this paragraph, Shabbat is compared to an inheritance. In English, it says "Grant that we inherit your holy gift of Shabbat." In Hebrew, it says:

וְהַנְחִילֵנוּ ה׳ אֱלֹהֵינוּ בְּאַהֲבָה וּבְרָצוֹן שַׁבַּת קָדְשֶׁךָ

<u>Let's think about the notion of inheritance, which is a special kind of gift. Do any of you know anything about inheritances? What is an inheritance?</u>

The dictionary definition of inheritance is: "possession of something as one's birthright; something received from parents or ancestors."

Now that you know something about inheritances in general, I'd like you to take out a piece of paper and try to answer the following question: How is the Shabbat like an inheritance?

When students finish writing, share some of their answers. You can do this sharing just by asking students who want to read their answers aloud to do so or by using a secret sharing technique.

Closing

Let's conclude our lesson for today by summarizing what we already know about the Shabbat Amidah.

List answers on the board. List should include:

it has seven berakhot

the first three and last three berakhot are the same as in the weekday Amidah

the middle berakha is called קְדֻשַּׁת הַיוֹם

its חֲתִימָה is בָּרוּךְ אַתָּה ה׳ מְקַדֵּשׁ הַשַּׁבָּת

in every Shabbat service, the middle berakha is different

the Shabbat is compared to an inheritance

it's important to rest on Shabbat

observing mitzvot makes us holy

Great list. It summarizes what makes the Shabbat Amidah different from the weekday Amidah, and it also lists those elements that the Amidah of each of the Shabbat services has in common. Now we're ready to discover what makes each Amidah different. Next time, we will continue studying other sections of the berakhot called קְדֻשַּׁת הַיוֹם.

Lesson Two

Materials: A chart that you can xerox and a chart with the correct answers can be found at the end of the lesson.

Setting The Stage

Last time when we discussed the Amidah for Shabbat, we read the paragraph from the berakha called קְדֻשַּׁת הַיּוֹם that is identical in each Shabbat service. Today, we will focus on the paragraphs that are unique to each service.

I'm going to give each of you a chart to fill in as we study. Filling in the chart will help keep us together and will help us figure out the ways in which each version of the Amidah is unique.

Lesson

Let's start with the קְדֻשַּׁת הַיּוֹם berakha in the Amidah for Erev Shabbat. You can find it on pages 298-299 in Siddur Sim Shalom and on page 22 in the Silverman Sabbath and Festival Prayer Book.

With what words does the berakha begin? Find them in Hebrew.

Read aloud the first few words in Hebrew.

What do those words mean? (You made the seventh day holy.)

Just based on those few opening words, what do you think the main idea of this paragraph of the berakha will be?

(holiness of the Shabbat)

Now read the paragraph in English.

How might you summarize the paragraph?

(God has made the seventh day special, different, from all the other days of the week.)

So you were right, the main idea of this paragraph is holiness.

Read the next paragraph in English and in Hebrew. Do you recognize it? Where is it from?

(It's from בְּרֵאשִׁית, from the very beginning of Genesis. It's the beginning of Kiddush for Friday evening.)

If you were not familiar with the וַיְכֻלּוּ passage, how would you know it was from the Torah?

(The end of the previous paragraph says, "as it is written in Your Torah.")

And what does the Torah text actually say about the seventh day?

(It describes how God stopped working on the seventh day and blessed the day itself and made it holy and unique.)

According to this berakha, what is the source of the specialness, the holiness of the Shabbat?

(At the beginning of time, God created the seventh day and set it apart from the rest of the days and blessed it and made it holy.)

Great work. Now let's take our charts and answer the questions asked about the berakha קְדֻשַׁת הַיוֹם for Friday night.

Give students time to fill out their charts. Check on the answers so you are sure everyone's answers are correct and then move on to study the next berakha.

Let's now study the same berakha in the Shaharit service. You'll find it on pages 358-359 in Siddur Sim Shalom and on page 98 in the Silverman Sabbath and Festival Prayer Book.

With what Hebrew words does the berakha begin?

(יִשְׂמַח מֹשֶׁה בְּמַתְּנַת חֶלְקוֹ)

What do those words mean?

(Moses was happy with his gift.)

Can you guess the idea of Shabbat that will be expressed in this paragraph based on the opening words. Hint: what was Moses's gift?

(Torah)

Read the first paragraph of this berakha in English.

What does it actually talk about?

(Moses receiving the Ten Commandments)

This paragraph ends with exactly the same words as the first paragraph of this berakha on Friday evening. What are those words?

Find them in Hebrew and in English.

(Thus it is written in Your Torah; וְכֵן כָּתוּב בְּתוֹרָתֶךְ)

Again the words, thus it is written in Your Torah tell us that we are going to find the idea that was just expressed in a quotation from the Torah.

If you were going to guess where the quotation from the Torah would come from, what would you guess?

(answers could include any suggestions that referred to the Jewish people receiving the Torah)

Read the quotation. It comes form Exodus 31:16-17. What does it say?

(Children of Israel should observe the Shabbat as a sign between them and God, and as a reminder of the Creation.)

What theme is included here that was also included in the קְדֻשַׁת הַיוֹם for Erev Shabbat?

(theme of Shabbat as a reminder of the creation)

What new ideas does this berakha add about the Shabbat?

(The importance of observing Shabbat and the idea that the Shabbat is a sign between God and the children of Israel.)

What do you think it means that the Shabbat is a sign between God and the children of Israel? What does it mean to be a sign between two parties? Can you think of examples of things that serve as signs of relationships between two people?

(engagement and wedding rings, presents like flowers)

What do these signs represent?

(something about the relationship, perhaps a sign of affection or caring)

Just as a ring can symbolize a relationship between two people, so does the Shabbat symbolize the relationship between God and the people of Israel.

Does the berakha say anything about how we are to observe Shabbat?

(no)

O.K. That's right. It just says that we should.

Read the words again in Hebrew. Perhaps you recognize these words. When else have you heard them?

(They are the words of the Kiddush that we recite on Shabbat at lunch)

If none recognizes the words, just fill in the information for them.

Now, let's take a few minutes to fill in our charts where it says Shaharit.

Now, let's study the middle berakha for Musaf. You can find it on pages 140-142 in the Silverman Sabbath and Festival Prayer Book and on pages 434-437 in Siddur Sim Shalom.

With what Hebrew words does the text begin?

(תִּקַּנְתָּ שַׁבָּת רָצִיתָ קָרְבְּנוֹתֶיהָ)

Do you recognize any of these words?

They may or may not recognize words in this paragraph.

Read the first phrase in English. It will give you a clue to the contents of this berakha. What's it going to be about?

(sacrifices)

Read the first two paragraphs in English. What are they saying?

(they talk about the sacrifices. They ask that we be able to again worship in Israel.)

Is there a quotation from the Torah that is part of this berakha?

(yes)

How do you know?

(it says "as written in Your Torah...")

What is the quotation from the Torah about?

(sacrificial offerings)

So one of the new things we learn in this Amidah is that during the time of the Temple, there was a special sacrificial ceremony unique to Shabbat. When we recite the Amidah for Musaf, we are recalling that ceremony.

What about the paragraph right after the quotation from the Torah, what is it about?

Read it first in English in order to answer the question.

(those that celebrate the Shabbat enjoy God's goodness. Shabbat as a reminder of creation.)

What do you think this means--those that celebrate the Shabbat enjoy God's goodness?

(somehow Shabbat is associated with being almost like a present from God, or if not a present than an expression of God's goodness to the people Israel.)

Can you think of any reasons that people would describe the Shabbat that way?

(maybe because it is such a special time, different from all the other days of the week.)

41

And again, we have the idea of Shabbat as a reminder of creation.

Read this paragraph in which Shabbat is called a reminder of the creation in Hebrew. Although it is not part of any Kiddush, you may recognize this paragraph. You may have sung it at camp or at the synagogue or in one of the other classes in religious school.

Again, let's fill in our charts.

Now let's turn to the Amidah for Minha. Can someone find the middle berakha, קְדֻשַׁת הַיּוֹם?

> (it's on pages 578-579 in Siddur Sim Shalom and on pages 171-172 in the Silverman Sabbath and Festival Prayer Book.

With what Hebrew words does it begin?

> (אַתָּה אֶחָד וְשִׁמְךָ אֶחָד)

What do you think this berakha is going to be about?

> (something about God and God's oneness)

Read the first paragraph of this berakha in English. What does this paragraph seem to be about?

> (God is unique, the people Israel is unique. The Shabbat that God has given us is perfect.)

Our commentators recognize the same themes that you have mentioned. They read into the paragraph a reference to the peace of the messianic era and of the spiritual world to come which is pictured in rabbinic literature as a time which has a Shabbat-like quality.

Do you have any ideas about how they could have given this kind of interpretation to this paragraph?

> (open ended question. Answers could include such notions as emphasis on oneness and perfection)

At this point ask students to fill in their charts for the Minha service.

Once students have finished their work, ask them to read back over their charts, and ask

What time in the history of the Jewish people does each berakha recall?

List their answers on the board. The board should look like this:

> creation
>
> time of giving and receiving of Torah

time of Temple sacrifices

Messianic time in the future

When we recite the Amidah for Shabbat, we, the Jewish people, reconnect ourselves with key times in our history. It is almost as though we review our past history and hopes for the future each and every week.

<u>Now let's look back at our charts again. This time let's look at the themes that we've focused on. What do they teach about the Shabbat?</u>

the Shabbat reminds us of the creation of the world

the Shabbat is a sign between God and the Jewish people

we are supposed to observe the Shabbat

during Temple times, there was a special observance of Shabbat in the Temple itself

we hope for a time in the future when each and every day will be as peaceful and perfect as Shabbat.

We started this unit by saying that we could learn a lot about Shabbat from the fact that each of these Amidot dealt with different content and I think the charts and lists that we've just made confirm this.

Closing

In order to summarize our work, we're going to make a mural that tells the story of the four different versions of the Amidah for Shabbat. The mural will have four sections: one for each of the berakhot that we've studied. Each of you can contribute your ideas to one of these four sections.

Either assign students to groups based on their ability to work together or allow students to choose based on their preference for thematic content. Working on the mural may involve some time from the next lesson. Even so, the questions that conclude this unit and which might follow students' mural work are included at this point.

When students conclude their work, ask the class members to look at the whole mural and just coment. Then ask them some of the following questions:

<u>Did you choose different colors to represent different themes?</u>

<u>How would you describe each section if you were trying to say something about its mood?</u>

This is a mural about קְדֻשַׁת הַיּוֹם, the uniqueness, the holiness, the specialness of Shabbat. Looking at it as a whole, how might you characterize the kedusha of Shabbat?

Where are we in this picture?

This last question is a crucial one. Students, we hope, will be able to express the thought that we enter the picture each Shabbat as we celebrate Shabbat; or we enter the picture as we recite the words of the berakhot; or we enter the picture as we paint it...which is another way of saying the same thing.

Chart for Students

Theme:	Time setting mentioned:	Hebrew words that begin Torah quote:	Hebrew words that begin Kedushat Hayom:	Service:

Filled-in Chart (for teachers)

Theme:	Time setting mentioned:	Hebrew words that begin Torah quote:	Hebrew words that begin Kedushat Hayom:	Service:
Reminder of creation	Creation	"וַיְכֻלּוּ"	"אַתָּה קִדַּשְׁתָּ"	שַׁבָּת עַרְבִית עֲמִידָה
Sign between God and Israel	Giving of Torah	"וְשָׁמְרוּ"	"יִשְׂמַח מֹשֶׁה"	שַׁחֲרִית
Joy that comes to those who observe Shabbat	Time of the Temple	"וּבְיוֹם הַשַּׁבָּת"	"תִּכַּנְתָּ שַׁבָּת"	מוּסָף
Perfection, oneness	Messianic Age	——	"אַתָּה אֶחָד"	מִנְחָה

HANUKKAH

Overview

In this lesson, students examine the concept miracle. They arc introduced to a definition of miracle found in Martin Buber's book, <u>Moses: the Revelation and the Covenant</u>, (Harper Torchbooks, Harper and Row, New York, 1958 edition). According to Buber, "miracle is simply what happens; in so far as it meets people who are capable of receiving it." (p. 7). In other words, a miracle is in the eyes of the beholder. Thus, if one perceives an event as miraculous—be it childbirth, the sunset, the Israelites' crossing of the Sea of Reeds, the recapture of Jerusalem in 1967—then, the event is a miracle. If, on the other hand, one experiences these very same events and does not perceive them with wonder and awe, then, according to Buber's definition, these events are not miracles for the individual.

One of the issues facing students in the Dalet-Hey years of religious school is organizing that which they have learned as younger children into a coherent world view. Their overwhelming sense of religious teaching is: "It's for kids," "no one really believes anything like that." Buber's definition is appealing because it accounts for miracles in a way that allows students to *personally reject* an event as miraculous while *accepting* that others could understand the event as a miracle.

In this lesson, students explore the concept "miracle," defining it themselves, and comparing and contrasting their definition with Buber's. They then examine three Siddur texts added to the liturgy on Hanukkah which mention miracles: 1) The Al Hanissim, עַל הַנִּסִּים, a paragraph added to the Amidah and Birkat HaMazon, 2) The second berakha recited when we light the Hanukkah lights, and 3) Hanerot Hallalu, הַנֵּרוֹת הַלָּלוּ,—the paragraph recited immediately following candle lighting. They also look again at the Modim (מוֹדִים)—the context of the עַל הַנִּסִּים—which also refers to miracles. Through this text study, students will discover ways in which the term "miracle" is used in the liturgy.

Students discover that although each of these texts talks about miracles, in no text is the nature of the miracle spelled out. That is, עַל הַנִּסִּים begins with the words "for the miracles," but what these miracles are is not mentioned -- at least not yet. The berakha שֶׁעָשָׂה נִסִּים refers to the miracles done for our ancestors. Again, the text

does not specify what the nature of these miracles is. The term miracles, or נִסִּים,
generally appears in the text without a referent. We, the reader, the worshipper must
fill in the referent. Therefore *our personal definition of miracle becomes critical* in how
we read the text. It is our definition that informs what we are saying and intending.
The lesson ends by asking students to think about the definitions of miracle that they
have discussed and choose the one that makes the most sense to them.

Materials: Buber's definition of miracles can be found at end of lesson and needs
to be xeroxed for student use.

Setting the Stage

Step #1   Pass out 3 x 5 cards. Ask students to write a definition of a miracle.

Step #2   When they have finished writing definitions, ask them to turn their cards
over and write an example of something they consider to be a miracle.

Step #3   Ask students who wish to share their definition to do so. Write definitions
in abbreviated form on the board.

Step #4   Do the same for the examples—writing several examples on the board that
students give share. Examples should be specific so if students respond
generally, with answers like Hanukkah; ask—to what specifically are you
referring?

Lesson

Now that we've shared some of our ideas about miracles, we're going to read a
definition of miracle suggested by a famous 20th century Jewish philosopher,
Martin Buber.

Pass out definition at this point.

The definition of miracle found in the lesson is an excerpt from Buber's book,
Moses. You will need to decide how much of the selection found at the end of this
lesson you want your students to read. The following sentence contains the essential
information.

"The concept of miracle which is permissible from the historical approach can
be defined at its starting point as an abiding astonishment. . . .Miracle is simply
what happens; in so far as it meets people who are capable of receiving it, or
are prepared to receive it as a miracle." (Martin Buber, *Moses,* pp. 75-78.)

Ask students to read the selection and to underline Buber's definition of miracle.

What is a miracle according to Buber? Find the words he used in the text and read them aloud.

Restate his definition in your own words?

(The key element here is: that people need to understand an event as miraculous or "wonderful" in order for that event to be considered a miracle.)

Write the definition as restated on the board in the column with the definitions of miracles.

Now ask students to examine all the definitions on the board and to try to categorize them.

The important steps in this categorizing exercise include:

students inspect the definitions on the board

students analyze similarities and differences

students group definitions into categories or comprehensive definitions.

Depending upon what's on the board, the categories or wording of categories may differ.

Two probable categories or comprehensive definitions will probably emerge:

miracle as <u>supernatural</u> (out of the ordinary/ above or beyond nature)

miracle as <u>point of view</u>: miracle as an event that is considered to be a miracle because that is how participants in the event experienced it.

Now that we've talked about miracles in general, let's turn our attention to Hanukkah—and its miracles. You've probably heard people refer to the miracle of Hanukkah, even popular news paper articles use the term miracle when describing Hanukkah. The Siddur also talks about Hanukkah and its miracles. Let's examine the Siddur texts in light of today's discussion on miracles.

The first text that we're going to examine is the עַל הַנִּסִּים. You can find it in your Siddurim on p. 116-117 in Siddur Sim Shalom; p. 100 in Silverman prayerbook.

A xeroxed copy of the עַל הַנִּסִּים is included at the end of this lesson. The translation is from *Seasons of Our Joy* by Arthur Waskow. It is preferable for students to use the Siddur that is regularly used in class.

On Hanukkah, the עַל הַנִּסִּים paragraph is added to the Amidah (עֲמִידָה) and to the Birkat HaMazon (בִּרְכַּת הַמָּזוֹן).

Please read it in English.

<u>In what time period are the events in the text set?</u>

    (Days of Mattathias.)

<u>What is described?</u>

Perhaps create a list on the board.

    (War, cleaning of Temple, lighting Hanukkah (חֲנֻכָּה) lights.)

<u>How is the war or military event described?</u>

    (Few conquered many, God stood up for Jewish people.)

<u>Who are the few? Who are the many?</u>

    (Jewish people who followed Mattathias and his son = few; Greeks were the many.)

You can ask this question in terms of several other descriptors as well: who were the guilty? who were the innocent, etc.?

<u>Once the military battles were over, what happened?</u>

    (The Jews came back, cleansed the Temple, kindled lights and set aside 8 days as a season for thanksgiving.)

<u>Now that we've looked at some of the contents of the עַל הַנִּסִּים, think of it as a whole. How does the עַל הַנִּסִּים answer the question: why do we celebrate Hanukkah?</u>

    (Basically because there was a military victory in which Jews were victorious.)

<u>According to the text, how did the holiday actually come into being?</u>

    (After the victory, the Jewish people set aside a special time to commemorate the event.)

<u>The words עַל הַנִּסִּים mean "because of the miracles." Examine the text again. Give examples of happenings that are described here which could be described as miracles.</u>

    (Many in hands of few, You delivered us, etc.)

Write these in the column of examples of miracles which are already on the board

<u>How do these examples seem to fit into the categories of miracles we already decided upon?</u>

<u>Are these supernatural occurrences/or are these events miracles because that's how they were experienced by those who participated in the events?</u>

Students can really answer this question either way. Some may say that these are examples of supernatural occurrences; others may say that these are miracles because the people involved experienced them as (a) miracle(s). Some students may try to create a definition of miracle that somehow combines both these definitions. Student need not agree on one answer. It's the discussion itself that is important. Once they have come to a conclusion, or agreed to disagree, give students the worksheet that is included at the end of this lesson. It includes three texts: the second berakha of the berakhot recited when lighting the חֲנֻכִּיָּה, the הַנֵּרוֹת הַלָּלוּ, the additional section recited when we complete the lighting of the חֲנֻכִּיָּה, and the מוֹדִים—the berakha to which the עַל הַנִּסִּים is added. In each case, students are asked to read the text and answer the question: what miracles are referred to in this text? Students can be asked to do this either as individuals or in small groups. If students have difficulty getting started, you may want to do the first text שֶׁעָשָׂה נִסִּים together with them.

Students will discover something very interesting.

In no case are specific miracles mentioned by name. In the בְּרָכָה recited when lighting the חֲנֻכִּיָּה, we are referred to "the miracles which God did for our ancestors at this season in ancient times." In the הַנֵּרוֹת הַלָּלוּ, the miracles according to the translation in Siddur Sim Shalom are the victories themselves; if translated more literally as in the Waskow translation, miracles have no referent in the text. The reader is left in the position of filling in the blank: the miracle referred to here is. . . . Because this selection is recited while looking at the חֲנֻכִּיָּה and because of the reference to the כֹּהֲנִים, one might assume that the miracle referred to is the one associated with the oil. In the מוֹדִים, the phrase is—"for your miracles which daily attend us." When the מוֹדִים has been taught as part of this curriculum (in kittah gimmel), we talked about everyday miracles from a Buberian point of view, that is being able to see the world around us as being filled with the "wonder"ful, with the miraculous. Again, miracle has no specific referent.

When students have completed their worksheets, ask them to share what they have found out. You may want them to first compare their answers with another student's answers before the class as a whole shares. For each text, the sharing should include two parts:

a. pointing out where they found the word 'miracle.'

b. a realization that miracle in these texts has no specific referent.

<u>**Now we all know that when people talk about Hanukkah they talk about miracles, what are they talking about?**</u>

(Probable answer: miracle of oil.)

51

<u>Did you read about that miracle in any of the Siddur texts?</u> (no)

The account of the oil does *not* come from Books of the Maccabees, the historical account of the origin of Hanukkah or from the Siddur. It does come from the Talmud. The rabbis of the Talmud are discussing "why Hanukkah" just as we are. And the answer they gave has become very famous "when the Maccabees went back to the Temple they only found enough oil sealed with the seal of the כֹּהֵן גָּדוֹל to kindle the Temple מְנוֹרָה for one day. This oil lasted for eight days. . . . sufficient time for a new oil supply to be made."

<u>Looking back at our two definitions of miracle(see page 49 above), which kind of miracle is the miracle of the oil?</u>

(supernatural kind)

<u>What kind of miracles are described in עַל הַנִּסִּים?</u>

(Either supernatural and point of view or just point of view.)

<u>What kind of miracles are described in מוֹדִים?</u>

(Depends on students reading of text—could be both supernatural and point of view or just point of view.)

<u>What about in הַנֵּרוֹת הַלָּלוּ and in the berakha?</u>

(We don't know because no specific miracle is mentioned.)

<u>Why do you think the miracle of the oil became a more famous reason for celebrating the holiday of Hanukkah than the miracle of the military victory described in the עַל הַנִּסִּים and the Book of the Maccabees?</u>

(This is an open ended question. Reasons might include, oil story is more miraculous; oil story is more appealing because it feels like it involves the supernatural; some people may think celebrating a military victory is wrong; we don't think of military victories as miracles.)

Closing

Now, let's look back at your original 3x5 card of your example of a miracle, how does it fit into these definitions of kinds of miracles.

<u>Which of the definitions of miracle do you personally prefer? Why?</u>

This last question could be phrased in the form of a sentence whip "The definition of miracle that I prefer is . . . because. . . ."

Students' answers will be subjective and students don't all have to agree on the "right" answer. They only need examine their own examples and decide on an answer that makes sense to them.

You may want to conclude the lesson by reading the Walt Whitman poem, "Miracles" (included at the end of this lesson). At the conclusion of the reading, you might want to ask students, **which of the definitions of miracle is closer to Whitman's,** or you may just want to read the poem and have no discussion afterward.

Appendix

Reading from: <u>Moses</u> by Martin Buber, Harper Torchbooks, Harper and Row: New York. pp. 75-76, and 77.

<u>What is decisive with respect to the inner history of Mankind, however, is that the children of Israel understood this as an act of God, as a "miracle;" which does not mean that they interpreted it as a miracle, but that they experienced it as such,</u> that as such they perceived it. This perception at the fateful hour, which is assuredly to be attributed largely to the personal influence of Moses, had a decisive influence on the coming into being of what is called "Israel" in the history of the spirit; on the development of the element "Israel" in the religious history of humanity.

The concept of miracle which is permissible from the historical approach can be defined at its starting point as <u>an abiding astonishment</u>. The philosophizing and the religious person both wonder at the phenomenon, but the one neutralizes his wonder in ideal knowledge, while the other abides in that wonder; no knowledge, no cognition, can weaken his astonishment. Any causal explanation only deepens the wonder for him. The great turning-points in religious history are based on the fact that again and ever again an individual and a group attached to him wonder and keep on wondering; at a natural phenomenon, at a historical event, or at both together; always at something which intervenes fatefully in the life of this individual and this group. They sense and experience it as a wonder. This, to be sure, is only the starting-point of the historical concept of wonder, but it cannot be explained away. Miracle is not something "supernatural" or "superhistorical," but an incident, an event which can be fully included in the objective, scientific nexus of nature and history; the vital meaning of which, however, for the person to whom it occurs, destroys the security of the whole nexus of knowledge for him, and <u>explodes the fixity of the fields of experience named "Nature" and "History." Miracle is simply what happens; in so far as it meets people who are capable of receiving it, or prepared to receive it as a miracle.</u> The extraordinary element favours this coming together, but it is not characteristic of it; the normal and ordinary can also undergo a transfiguration into miracle in the light of the suitable hour...

It is irrelevant whether "much" or "little," unusual things or usual tremendous or trifling events happened; what is vital is only that what happened was experienced, while it happened, as the act of God. The people saw in whatever it was they saw "the great hand," and they "believed in YHVH," or, more correctly translated, they gave their trust to YHVH.

We have found that the permissible concept of miracle from the historical approach means, to begin with, nothing but an abiding astonishment. In order to arrive at the completeness of the miracle from this concept we must add something which proves to be essential. We may ascribe what gives rise to our astonishment to a specific power, which therefore requires no other content than that of being the doer of this miracle or this kind of miracle, than to be, so to say, the subject of a miracle. That does not do away with the astonishment, the event is not included in a general chain of cause and effect apt to explain it adequately; but for the performance of the miracle a particular magical spirit, a special demon, a special idol is called into being. It is an idol just because it is special. But that is not what historical consideration means by miracle. For where a doer is restricted by other doers, the current system of cause and effect is replaced by another, less adequate, lacking sequence and connection. The real miracle means that in the astonishing experience of the event the current system of cause and effect becomes, as it were, transparent and permits a glimpse of the sphere in which sole power, not restricted by any other, is at work. To live with the miracle means to recognize this power on every given occasion as the effecting one. That is the religion of Moses...

TEXT FOR STUDENTS

On Ḥanukkah:

עַל הַנִּסִּים וְעַל הַפֻּרְקָן, וְעַל הַגְּבוּרוֹת, וְעַל הַתְּשׁוּעוֹת, וְעַל
הַמִּלְחָמוֹת שֶׁעָשִׂיתָ לַאֲבוֹתֵינוּ בַּיָּמִים הָהֵם וּבַזְּמַן הַזֶּה.

בִּימֵי מַתִּתְיָהוּ בֶּן־יוֹחָנָן כֹּהֵן גָּדוֹל, חַשְׁמוֹנַי וּבָנָיו, כְּשֶׁעָמְדָה
מַלְכוּת יָוָן הָרְשָׁעָה עַל עַמְּךָ יִשְׂרָאֵל לְהַשְׁכִּיחָם תּוֹרָתֶךָ וּלְהַעֲבִירָם
מֵחֻקֵּי רְצוֹנֶךָ, וְאַתָּה בְּרַחֲמֶיךָ הָרַבִּים עָמַדְתָּ לָהֶם בְּעֵת צָרָתָם,
רַבְתָּ אֶת־רִיבָם, דַּנְתָּ אֶת־דִּינָם, נָקַמְתָּ אֶת־נִקְמָתָם, מָסַרְתָּ גִבּוֹרִים
בְּיַד חַלָּשִׁים, וְרַבִּים בְּיַד מְעַטִּים, וּטְמֵאִים בְּיַד טְהוֹרִים, וּרְשָׁעִים
בְּיַד צַדִּיקִים, וְזֵדִים בְּיַד עוֹסְקֵי תוֹרָתֶךָ. וּלְךָ עָשִׂיתָ שֵׁם גָּדוֹל
וְקָדוֹשׁ בְּעוֹלָמֶךָ, וּלְעַמְּךָ יִשְׂרָאֵל עָשִׂיתָ תְּשׁוּעָה גְדוֹלָה וּפֻרְקָן
כְּהַיּוֹם הַזֶּה. וְאַחַר כֵּן בָּאוּ בָנֶיךָ לִדְבִיר בֵּיתֶךָ וּפִנּוּ אֶת־הֵיכָלֶךָ,
וְטִהֲרוּ אֶת־מִקְדָּשֶׁךָ, וְהִדְלִיקוּ נֵרוֹת בְּחַצְרוֹת קָדְשֶׁךָ, וְקָבְעוּ
שְׁמוֹנַת יְמֵי חֲנֻכָּה אֵלּוּ לְהוֹדוֹת וּלְהַלֵּל לְשִׁמְךָ הַגָּדוֹל.

Hebrew text from <u>Siddur Sim Shalom</u> edited by Rabbi Jules Harlow (New York: The Rabbinical Assembly, 1985)

On account of the miracles and the deliverance, the triumphs and liberations and battles that you accomplished for our forebears in these days at this season--It was in the days of Mattathias, son of Yokhanan, the Hasmonean high priest, and his sons that there arose the evil Hellenistic empire to rule over Your people Israel, to force them to forget Your Torah and to violate the rulings that You willed. But You in in Your great motherly compassion stood up to side with them and plead their case in their time of trouble. You delivered the mighty into the hand of the weak, the many into the hand of the few, those soaked in death into the hand of the pure, the wicked into the hand of the righteous, the arrogant into the hand of those who pore over Your Torah. For Yourself You made a great and holy Name in all the worlds, and Your people Israel You made a great and liberating deliverance, till this very day. And after all that, Your children came to the shrine of Your house to cleanse Your Temple and purify Your holy place, to kindle lights in Your holy courtyards and to establish these eight days of Hanukkah so as to thank and praise Your great Name.

English translation from <u>Seasons of Our Joy</u> by Arthur Waskow (Bantam Books, 1982), p. 97.

Miracles
by Walt Whitman

Why, who makes much of a miracle?

As to me I know of nothing else but miracles,

Whether I walk the streets of Manhattan,

Or dart my sight over the roofs of houses toward the sky,

Or wade with naked feet along the beach just in the edge of the
   water

Or stand under trees in the woods,

Or talk by day with any one I love, or sleep in the bed at night
   with any one I love,

Or sit at table at dinner with the rest,

Or look at strangers opposite me riding in the car,

Or watch honey-bees busy around the hive of a summer forenoon,

Or animals feeding in the fields,

Or birds, or the wonderfulness of insects in the air,

Or the wonderfulness of the sundown, or of stars shining so
   quiet and bright,

Or the exquisite delicate thin curve of the new moon in spring;

These with the rest, one and all, are to me miracles,

The whole referring, yet each distinct and in its place.

To me every hour of the light and dark is a miracle,

Every cubic inch of space is a miracle,

Every square yard of the surface of the earth is spread with the
   same,

Every foot of the interior swarms with the same.

To me the sea is a continual miracle,
The fishes that swim--the rocks--the motion of the waves--the
   ships with men in them,
What stranger miracles are there?

from <u>Leaves of Grass</u> (last edition)

בָּרוּךְ אַתָּה יְיָ אֱלֹהֵינוּ מֶלֶךְ הָעוֹלָם, שֶׁעָשָׂה נִסִּים לַאֲבוֹתֵינוּ בַּיָּמִים הָהֵם וּבַזְּמַן הַזֶּה.

Praised are You, Lord our God, King of the universe who accomplished miracles for our ancestors in ancient days, and in our time.

What Miracles are referred to in this text

Chart for Students (Part Two)

After lighting the lights:

לָכֵן, מוּאָרִים אָנוּ לָכֵן מֵהֶם עַל ...

After lighting the lights:

These lights we kindle to recall the wondrous triumphs and the miraculous victories wrought through Your holy kohanim for our ancestors in ancient days at this season. These lights are sacred through all the eight days of Hanukkah. We may not put them to ordinary use, but are to look upon them and thus be reminded to thank and praise You for the wondrous miracle of our deliverance.

What Miracles are referred to in this text

60

Chart for Students (Part Three)

מוֹדִים אֲנַחְנוּ לָךְ שָׁאַתָּה הוּא יְיָ אֱלֹהֵינוּ וֵאלֹהֵי אֲבוֹתֵינוּ לְעוֹלָם וָעֶד, צוּר חַיֵּינוּ מָגֵן יִשְׁעֵנוּ אַתָּה הוּא לְדוֹר וָדוֹר. נוֹדֶה לְּךָ וּנְסַפֵּר תְּהִלָּתֶךָ עַל חַיֵּינוּ הַמְּסוּרִים בְּיָדֶךָ, וְעַל נִשְׁמוֹתֵינוּ הַפְּקוּדוֹת לָךְ, וְעַל נִסֶּיךָ שֶׁבְּכָל יוֹם עִמָּנוּ, וְעַל נִפְלְאוֹתֶיךָ וְטוֹבוֹתֶיךָ שֶׁבְּכָל עֵת, עֶרֶב וָבֹקֶר וְצָהֳרָיִם, הַטּוֹב כִּי לֹא כָלוּ רַחֲמֶיךָ, וְהַמְרַחֵם כִּי לֹא תַמּוּ חֲסָדֶיךָ, מֵעוֹלָם קִוִּינוּ לָךְ.	We proclaim that You are the Lord our God and God of our ancestors throughout all time. You are the Rock of our lives, the Shield of our salvation in every generation. We thank You and praise You morning, noon, and night for Your miracles which daily attend us and for Your wondrous kindnesses. Our lives are in Your hand; our souls are in Your charge. You are good, with everlasting mercy; You are compassionate, with enduring lovingkindness. We have always placed our hope in You.	What Miracles are referred to in this text

TU BISHVAT

Overview

Although there are no additions to the daily liturgy unique to Tu Bishvat, the holiday itself serves to remind us of our personal connection to Eretz Yisrael and to the wonders of the natural world. Holidays often express in a unique, "once a year" way, ideas that we think are very important. This is certainly the case for Tu Bishvat.

In this lesson, students study בִּרְכַּת הַשָּׁנִים, the ninth berakha of the daily Amidah, and Tu Bishvat as examples of a daily and a once-a-year way to remind ourselves of these two ideas--"the wonder in the ordinary" and our personal connection to Eretz Yisrael.

Materials

Photocopy selection from Waskow's <u>Seasons of our Joy</u>, found later in this lesson

Setting the Stage

<u>What does it mean to take things for granted?</u>

(not to notice them)

<u>Do you think it's good or bad to take things for granted? Explain your answer.</u>

(open-ended)

Today, we are going to discuss an everyday and a yearly way in which we as Jews remind ourselves not to take the wonders of the natural world for granted.

Lesson

Write on the board:

We Remind Ourselves Not To Take Things For Granted

1) Everyday Ways

Let's begin our lesson by creating a list of the everyday ways that we remind ourselves of the wonders of the natural world.

This activity can be done by the class as a whole or by small groups. In either case, list answers on the board. Hopefully, among the answers given will be some of the berakhot that students have learned in previous years. If students don't mention berakhot at all, you might ask them:

What berakhot have we learned that remind us of the wonders of the natural world?

These berakhot could include short berakhot like the הַמּוֹצִיא and בּוֹרֵא פְּרִי הָאֲדָמָה or a long berakha like the מוֹדִים. Students may also suggest other berakhot that they have learned for holidays or special occasions, for example, the berakha recited on seeing a rainbow. The latter are not berakhot that we recite every day. In responding to answers that include suggestions not possible every day, add an additional category to the listing on the board:

We Remind Ourselves Not To Take Things For granted

1) Everyday Ways   2) Special Occasions

We now have two lists on the board. One which includes everyday ways in which we remind ourselves not to take things for granted and one which includes special ways in which we remind ourselves not to take things for granted.

In the Amidah, we can find other "everyday examples" of berakhot that remind us not to take the natural world for granted. The מוֹדִים is one such example. Another is the ninth berakha of the Amidah, the berakha known as בִּרְכַּת הַשָּׁנִים. It begins with the words:

בָּרֵךְ עָלֵינוּ ה׳ אֱלֹהֵינוּ אֶת הַשָּׁנָה הַזֹּאת וְאֶת כָּל מִינֵי תְבוּאָתָהּ לְטוֹבָה and it ends with the hatimah:

בָּרוּךְ אַתָּה ה׳ , מְבָרֵךְ הַשָּׁנִים.

The berakha can be found in Siddur Sim Shalom on pp. 112-113, Silverman, p. 232.

Write the Hebrew words found above on the board.

If you examine only the seven words on the board, one word base or word root repeats three times. Which is it?

(בָּרֵךְ)

What other word do you know that has the same root or שֹׁרֶשׁ?

(בְּרָכָה)

Now read the berakha in Hebrew and English. What is its theme?

(good year, good harvest)

As far as you know, are there good and bad years for rains and harvests? Give some examples.

(years of drought, years of too much rain or snow)

There's one sentence that varies with the season of the year. Find it. What are the sentence phrases that change depending on the season of the year.?

How is each appropriate to the season in which it is to be recited?

(in the winter, when rain is needed, we say:וְתֵן טַל וּמָטָר לִבְרָכָה

in the summer, we say: וְתֵן בְּרָכָה)

Write these phrases on the board.

Saying this berakha each day is a way of reminding ourselves of the natural world and how much we need certain things to go right in order for it to be a good year.

So far, what things have we mentioned which need to go right for it to be a good year?

Create this list by implication from the berakha...e.g. sun, rain, seasonal temperatures etc.

There's one other time in the Amidah when we take notice of the natural world and remind ourselves not to take it for granted. I'll give you a clue, it's in the second berakha--and we don't say it all the time.

The second berakha of the Amidah can be found on pp. 106-107 in Siddur Sim Shalom; Silverman, p. 230.

Raise your hand if you have found the phrase that I'm referring to.

(It's מַשִּׁיב הָרוּחַ וּמוֹרִיד הַגֶּשֶׁם)

What does this phrase mean?

(You cause the wind to blow and the rain to fall)

When do we recite this phrase?

(between Shemini Atzeret, the seventh day of Sukkot, and Pesach)

65

<u>Why do you think that we recite it only then?</u>

(because that's the time of the rainy season in Israel)

<u>If you consider this phrase, what needs to go right for there to be a good year?</u>

(rain)

I'm going to add בִּרְכַּת הַשָּׁנִים and the phrase מַשִּׁיב הָרוּחַ וּמוֹרִיד הַגָּשֶׁם to our list of everyday times on the board.

<u>Often tefillot are everyday reminders and holidays are once a year reminders of the same ideas. What holidays can you think of that celebrate the natural world?</u>

(Sukkot and Tu Bishvat)

<u>What do Sukkot and Tu Bishvat have in common?</u>

(Both are tied to the growing season in Eretz Yisrael, both celebrate the growth of "nature."

<u>What is different about them?</u>

(Sukkot is celebrated as a "religious" holiday; going to the synagogue, berakhot recited while sitting in the sukkah and using the lulav and etrog.

Tu Bishvat has no "religious" ceremonies attached to it like synagogue, etc.; it does have a custom of having a Seder but that's a custom not a law.

<u>What do we do to celebrate Tu Bishvat?</u>

(Plant trees, buy trees in Israel.)

Tu Bishvat is celebrated in such a different way because it had such a different beginning as a holiday.

Distribute photocopy of the selection on the next page for students to read:

Reading: Tu Bishvat

"When the Temple still stood, one tenth of the income of the Israelite farmers and shepherds was taxed (tithed) for the support of the priesthood and of the poor. After the Temple was destroyed, the tithing system continued in the Land of Israel and for many Diaspora Jews. The income from the contributions went to those priests and Levites who were also Torah scholars and finally to students of Torah whether they were priests and Levites or not.

The tithing system included a one-tenth tax on fruit. The tithe of fruit could only be given on behalf of the fruit crop of a given year, out of the fruit that actually ripened in that year. So in order to organize the tithe correctly there had to be a tax year--an agreed upon date by which to define the end of the fruit crop of the previous year, and the beginning of the fruit crop of the next year. The date chosen for the new year in regard to fruit was Tu Bishvat, the fifteenth of the Hebrew month of Shvat."

(This information was taken from pages 105-106 of "Seasons of Our Joy", by Arthur Waskow, published by Bantam Books, 1982.)

After students read these paragraphs, ask them to explain the origin of Tu Bishvat as they understand it based on their reading.

It is interesting that a holiday like Tu Bishvat had a legal reason for its origin. It marked the beginning of the tax year for fruit. In the way we now celebrate and think about Tu Bishvat, its legal origin has almost been transformed. Rather than reminding us of taxes, it teaches us about the ideas that the prayers we have been studying want us to remember. That is, not to take the natural world for granted.

If the class is using the dalet holiday materials, it would be appropriate to add: These ideas and more are reflected in the Psalms that we will be studying in our green holiday books.

Closing

Today, we've been talking about the natural world and our tendency to take for granted the orderly, harmonious cycles of rain and dew and harvests. We've looked at the ways we remind ourselves to appreciate them.

In order to finish our lesson, let's look back at our two lists and see if we need to add anything now that we've thought more and talked more about these issues.

Now think about the בִּרְכַּת הַשָּׁנִים; are there any other words or phrases, in Hebrew or in English, that you can think of that would enhance the ideas of the berakha that are already there?

Now think about this coming Tu Bishvat. Can you think of something that we can do this year as individuals or as a class that can help us remind ourselves not to take the natural world for granted?

ROSH HODESH - TWO LESSONS

Overview

The purpose of this two lesson unit is to teach more about the Jewish calendar. Thus far, students have learned that the Jewish calendar is based on moon months, and they have dated the holidays according to these months. In some classes, there has been a regular opening ceremony in which the teacher asks students for the date on the Jewish calendar and notes it in a public way. Often the cycle and appearance of the moon are mentioned at this time as well.

In these lessons, students will focus on some of the intricacies of the Jewish calendar (the Jewish calendar is based on the cycles of the moon and on the rotation of the earth around the sun; the system of adding an additional month—אֲדָר שֵׁנִי—seven times in nineteen years so that the holidays based on the agricultural—solar—cycle will not float through the year) and on the custom of announcing the new moon publicly. This sequence can be taught before the beginning of any month. We are suggesting that it be taught before רֹאשׁ חֹדֶשׁ אֲדָר because אֲדָר is the key to keeping the lunar and solar cycles on track. In a leap year, it might be appropriate to teach the lesson before אֲדָר שֵׁנִי.

Lesson One

Materials: a photocopy of Biblical verses needed for this lesson can be found at the end of this lesson.

Setting the Stage

Place a variety of calendars on display . . . weekly, monthly, daily, yearly, Jewish, secular. Ask students to examine them and describe them:

<u>What is the same about all the objects and what is different about them?</u>

> (They are all calendars, they all mark time slightly differently in terms of how they are organized.)

<u>How would I find today's date?</u>

<u>What if I wanted to find the Jewish date?</u>

<u>What if I wanted to find ראש חדש or the first day of next month? What would I do?</u>

> (Look at a calendar.)

<u>How could you figure it out if you didn't have a calendar?</u>

> (Watch for the new moon.)

That's right. Because the Jewish calendar is based on the cycles of the moon. A lunar month, that is a month based on the moon's cycle, is 29½ days long. But because it would be complicated to make a month 29½ days, months were arbitrarily set at 29 or 30 days long.

Lesson

Today we're going to study more about the Jewish calendar and how it came to be. Let's begin by figuring out how many days a year based on 12 lunar months would have.

Set up the problem on the board: 29.5 x 12.

> (The answer is 354.)

<u>Does our year have 354 days?</u>

<u>How many days does it have?</u>

> (365.)

<u>Can anyone tell me why?</u>

> (It takes the earth 365 days to rotate around the sun.)

If students cannot answer, explain that our secular calendar is a solar calendar, that means that it is based on the sun.

<u>How does the earth's rotation around the sun affect our lives?</u>

(The seasons and the number of hours of sunlight are determined by this rotation.)

Actually, it takes the earth 365 1/4 days to go around the sun. But a calendar doesn't include 1/4 days any more than it includes 1/2 days. So every four years we add a day, February 29, to the year. The year with the added day is called a leap year.

The Jewish calendar also has leap years, but they are more complicated to figure out because the Jewish calendar is based on both cycles: that of the moon and that of the sun.

We're going to study three verses in the Torah to discover why.

If students have copies of the Torah, ask several students to look up one of the three verses. If not, xerox the verses. They can be found at the end of the lesson. Once students have located the verse, ask a volunteer to read each verse aloud. All of the verses mention that Pesah is supposed to come in the spring. The verses are Exodus 23:15; Exodus 34:18; and Deuteronomy 16:1

<u>Based on your reading, when is Pesah supposed to be each year?</u>

(Spring time in Israel.)

<u>Let's imagine that the Jewish calendar was only based on the lunar year. In our imaginary year, Pesah, which begins on the 14th of נִיסָן, which is a full moon, comes out on April 15. When would the 14th of נִיסָן come out the following year? (Hints: remember that we're imagining a life based on a lunar calendar. How many days less does a lunar year have from a solar year?)</u>

<u>So how would we figure this out?</u>

On board: April 15 minus 11 days equals April 4.

April 15

−11 days

_____

April 4

<u>What would happen the following year?</u>

April 4

−11 days

_____

March 24

71

<u>What about the next year?</u>

March 24

−11 days

_____

March 13

<u>If this continued, soon Pesah would be coming in February and then January. In light of the Torah verses you read, why would this be a problem?</u>

(Because Pesah has to come in the spring.)

In order to make certain that Pesah comes in the spring and Sukkot comes at the fall harvest time and Tu Bishvat comes at the beginning of tree planting time in Israel, the lunar months needed to fit the solar calendar. That's because the seasons are determined by solar cycles.

<u>What possible ways can you figure out to adjust the lunar calendar so that it will coincide with the solar calendar and the holidays will remain in their proper seasons?</u>

(Add 11 days at the end of each year; make some months longer.)

Both of these are possible solutions, but they couldn't work because the added 11 day month or the longer than 30 day month would not coincide with the moon's cycles.

Early on, the adjustment was made by occasionally adding an extra month whenever the cycles were moving too far apart. But then mathematicians figured out that after 19 years, the solar cycle would be 209 days longer than the lunar cycle. 11 days x 19 years equals 209 days or 7 months of thirty days which have 210 days in them. 30 days x 7 months = 210.

Put computations on board.

	19				30
x	11			x	7
---	---			---	---
	209				210

For these reasons, it was decided to add a month to the calendar 7 times every 19 years to keep the cycles more or less even. The additional month is added halfway through the year. It is called אֲדָר שֵׁנִי, a second אֲדָר.

If the year in which you're teaching this is a leap year, indicate the beginning of the month on their calendars.

Years in which there is an אֲדָר שֵׁנִי added are called leap years in the Jewish calendar.

Closing

Give students the pertinent data for the next Jewish lunar months, i.e., when is Rosh Hodesh, is it a month with 29 or 30 days, and ask them to create an accurate calendar. Ask them to use the Jewish month as the main organizing feature and add the secular dates to it. (You'll need to tell them on which day of the secular calendar the month begins.)

Biblical Verses

You shall obvserve the Feast of Unleavened Bread--eating unleavened bread for seven days as I have commanded you--at the set time in the month of Aviv, for in it you went forth from Egypt; and none shall appear before Me empty-handed...

(Exodus 23:15)

You shall observe the Feast of Unleavened Bread--eating unleavened bread for seven days, as I have commanded you--at the set time of the month of Aviv, for in the month of Aviv you went forth from Egypt.

(Exodus 34:18)

Observe the month of Aviv and offer a passover sacrifice to the Lord your God, for it was in the month of Aviv, at night, that the Lord you God freed you from Egypt.

(Deuteronomy 16:1)

Lesson Two

Setting the Stage

On the board before class begins, write the following statement. Include information pertaining to the coming month.

THIS IS AN ANNOUNCEMENT:

רֹאשׁ חֹדֶשׁ _____ WILL BE _____ AND

MAY IT COME TO US AND TO ALL ISRAEL FOR GOOD.

(Fill in the appropriate month and day in the blank spaces above)

<u>What is this announcement about?</u>

(When Rosh Hodesh will take place.)

<u>Why might I announce this to you?</u>

(So we would know when Rosh Hodesh will be.)

In the days of the Temple, before there was a set calendar, Rosh Hodesh was announced publicly. Two witnesses, who through careful looking, observed when there was no moon (or only the tiniest sliver of a moon), would come to the סַנְהֶדְרִין, the Jewish law court, and report what they had seen. Based on their observation, Rosh Hodesh, the beginning day of the new month was announced. That way, everyone began the month on the same day. That way, everyone celebrated holidays at the same time. Even though we now have a set calendar, we have continued this custom of announcing Rosh Hodesh publicly each month. The Shabbat before Rosh Hodesh, a special announcement is made in the synagogue about what day of the week Rosh Hodesh will be. This announcement is called בִּרְכַּת הַחֹדֶשׁ.

When the preceding month has 29 days, Rosh Hodesh has one day. When the preceding month has 30 days, Rosh Hodesh has 2 days. The first day is the 30th day of the preceding month; the second day is the first day of the new month.

If you were going to write a prayer that would be recited each month in the synagogue before Rosh Hodesh, what wishes and hopes for a good month would you include in it?

Either have students orally brainstorm a list or ask them to make a written list and then share it orally. During the oral sharing, list their wishes on the board. Then ask them to look at בִּרְכַּת הַחֹדֶשׁ on page 129 in the Silverman <u>Sabbath and Festival Prayerbook</u> or on page 418 in <u>Siddur Sim Shalom</u>.

Find the lines that are similar to the announcement on the board. I'll give you a clue to help you find them. They have blank lines in addition to the Hebrew words.

What's different about the words on the board and the words in the siddur?

Why are there blank spaces in the siddur (and on the board)?

How would we fill them in for the coming month?

Write the answer to the last question on the board in Hebrew. The board will now have the words (with the appropirate words filled in):

יְהְיֶה בְּיוֹם   רֹאשׁ חֹדֶשׁ

(There would be no blanks on the board, however.)

Now let's examine the first paragraph on this page closely.

Take a look at the opening words of the paragraph. What words tell you that this tefillah is connected to the new month?

(Renew this month _____.)

Which words in Hebrew have the same word base or שׁרֶשׁ?

What is the word base? What does it mean?

(New, חָדָשׁ.)

What kinds of connections can you think of between חֹדֶשׁ (month) and חָדָשׁ (new)?

(Each month there is a new moon.)

It's interesting that in English the word moon and month also seem to be related.

Now read the first paragraph in English. It includes the wishes and hopes for the new month. Let's make a list of the hopes and wishes found in the paragraph. (This could be a class activity or a small group activity). Let's compare the wishes that our class wrote and the wishes in this tefillah. Which ones are similar?

Optional activity: You may also want students to find the differences between their tefillah requests and the ones in the written prayer.

<u>Can you think of a tefillah that is similar to this paragraph that is said everyday?</u>

Because the paragraph is filled with requests, it might remind them of the middle berakhot of the Amidah.

Even if students cannot answer this question, continue by saying something like this:

<u>It also reminds me of the very last paragraph of the Amidah, the אֱלֹהַי נְצוֹר.</u>

If it is convenient, ask students to take out their siddurim and read over the אֱלֹהַי נְצוֹר.

As you may remember, last year you studied this paragraph. At that time you learned that the אֱלֹהַי נְצוֹר was the כַּוָּנָה or meditation that Mar, the son of Ravina, a rabbi who lived in Babylonia in the 4th century, recited at the conclusion of his recitation of the Amidah each day.

The paragraph that we have been studying -- בִּרְכַּת הַחֹדֶשׁ -- was originally the final כַּוָּנָה or meditation that Rav, the founder of the Babylonian Academy of Sura, a third century אֲמוֹרָא, used to recite at the conclusion of his recitation of the Amidah. Of course, when this כַּוָּנָה was recited at the end of the Amidah, it referred to the every day and not to the new month. Just as

אֱלֹהַי נְצוֹר, the personal כַּוָּנָה of Mar, the son of Ravina, was added to the Amidah and became the concluding paragraph that we all recite; so did this personal כַּוָּנָה of Rav become the way in which we all express our hopes and wishes for each new month!

Closing:

This year we've been talking about once a year prayers and everyday prayers. Today, we've learned a new kind of prayer, a once a month prayer.

<u>How would you summarize the contents of this prayer? Or, tell me in your own words what this tefillah is saying.</u> (Give time for discussion).

Some of the phrases remind me of Rosh Hashanah and Yom Kippur. Take another look at the first paragraph. Are there any words or phrases that seem to be asking for a good month in a way that remind you of Rosh Hashanah or Yom Kippur?

(Renew, long life, a life of peace, etc.)

In the same way that we ask for a good new year on Rosh Hashanah and Yom Kippur, we get a chance each month to ask for a good new month. This tefillah reminds us that each month we get a new chance, a new beginning.

To conclude our lesson today, I would like each of you to take out a piece of paper and write a brief summary of בִּרְכַּת הַחֹדֶשׁ. Then add some of your personal wishes for the coming month.

When students complete their work, you might take their papers and place them on a bulletin board that you could entitle: Our Wishes for the New Month.

HALLEL--preferably taught before Pesah

Overview

In this lesson, students compare a section of Birkat Geulah (the berakha which comes immediately after the Shema in Shaharit and Maariv) with a section of the Hallel. The subject of both texts is the experience of the Jewish people leaving Egypt.

In Birkat Geulah, the experience is recounted in a series of short verb clauses. The subject of each of these clauses is God; the object is the Jewish people; the verb describes God's action. In the Hallel, this same experience is recounted in a much more poetic way. The psalmist begins by setting the scene. It is the time when the Israelites are leaving Egypt. Then what is recounted is not the reaction of the Israelites to the experience, but a poetic account of how the world of nature responded to this extraordinary event.

In this lesson, students will analyze these very different ways of describing experiences. They will again use Buber's definition of miracle, this time, to understand the ways in which the Siddur discusses the Exodus. Finally, students will discuss the differences between descriptive and poetic language. One way to make meaning of the Hallel is to understand it as an expression of the miraculousness of the Exodus for those who actually experienced it.

Materials: photocopies of the second paragraph of Hallel and the Maariv Birkat Geulah paragraph from Siddur Sim Shalom (included at end of lesson)

Setting the Stage

Begin the lesson by asking:

Think of some very special events that have happened in your life or in your family's life.

Let's share some of the events that you have been thinking about.

After students have had the opportunity to share, ask:

Based on your verbal description, could we, your listeners, know how you or members of your family felt at the time this event happened?

(probably sometimes we could and sometimes we couldn't)

If you think we could, what elements in the account helped us?

(the excitement or enthusiasm of the telling, the accuracy of detail)

When we couldn't know how you felt, in what ways could you have added or changed your description, so that we could have known more about how you felt?

(perhaps, more detail could have been added to the account, more enthusiasm, more words that describe emotions)

A good way to summarize or crystallize the ideas that we have been discussing would be to imagine your bar or bat mitzvah. Imagine a newspaper account of it. And then,...imagine your mom's account of it. Tell me how those two accounts would be different.

Allow some time for sharing.

It's really interesting hearing your responses. It's clear that different ways of telling give us different feelings and even different understandings of an event.

Lesson

In the Siddur, we have a unique opportunity to study two accounts of a very special event in the life of the Jewish people. Today, we're going to study these two accounts and try to figure out how they are similar and how they are different.

For this lesson, we are suggesting that you use the text of Birkat Geulah in the Maariv service with the translation in Siddur Sim Shalom (ed. Jules Harlow). For your convenience, a photocopy of this text is found at the end of this lesson.

Let's begin by identifying the two texts. One is from Birkat Geulah, the berakha that we recite after the Shema. The other is from the Hallel, a special selection of Psalms recited on holidays.

Begin by scanning both texts. Tell me what event they both describe.

(Exodus, Israel's redemption from Egypt)

Find the references to the Exodus in each text and underline them.

Share answers.

In the Hallel, the opening words of the paragraph tell us that it's about the time when the Israelites left Egypt; in Birkat Geulah, it says "He vindicated us with miracles before Pharaoh" etc.

The theme, telling about the Exodus, is what these two texts have in common. Now let's take a closer look at each in order to find out how they are different from each other.

When groups complete their work, share responses. Begin with Birkat Geulah. You may want to begin the sharing by asking volunteers to read the selection aloud.

<u>Who is the subject of the paragraph?</u>

(God)

<u>What verbs are used to describe what God did?</u>

(redeems, delivers, brings judgement)

<u>For whom did God do all these things?</u>

(Israelites, Jewish people)

<u>Did the people experience this whole event as special?</u>

(yes)

<u>How do you know?</u>

(they sang praises to God)

<u>What words did they use to praise God?</u>

(the words: מִי כָמֹכָה בָּאֵלִם ה׳ , מִי כָּמֹכָה נֶאְדָּר בַּקֹּדֶשׁ, נוֹרָא תְהִלֹּת עֹשֵׂה פֶלֶא

and ה׳ יִמְלֹךְ לְעֹלָם וָעֶד)

Those verses are from the book of Exodus. They are the words that the Children of Israel sang after crossing the Sea and experiencing the power of God.

Using Buber's definition of miracle that we learned at Hanukkah, that is, "a miracle is an event experienced by those who participate in it as extraordinary or miraculous," **do you think that this text understands the Exodus as a miracle for the Jewish people?**

(yes)

<u>What's the miracle?</u>

(God's saving of the Jewish people when they were in trouble)

Now let's examine the paragraph of the Hallel.

Again, you may want to begin be asking someone to read it aloud.

<u>What are the subjects and verbs used in this paragraph?</u>

(Judah became holy, mountains leaped, sea fled, earth trembled)

How do you even know that these phrases refer to the Exodus?

(the paragraph begins with the words: "when the people Israel left Egypt")

Let me ask you, can mountains really leap? Or can the sea run? (No)

If these phrases are not meant to describe an event as it actually took place, how do you understand them? In other words, why do you think that the author chose these kinds of words to describe Israel's leaving Egypt?

(It was such a wonderful event, so fantastic, that regular words wouldn't do. Maybe this was the most powerful way that the author could describe how great this event was)

Maybe this was the way that the Siddur says, the whole earth went wild, rejoicing about what God did for our people.

Remember our discussion at the beginning of the lesson. We talked about sharing special events in our lives with others. We might think about the paragraph from the Hallel that we have been studying as an attempt to share a very emotional experience in a very vivid way using wild and impossible examples from the natural world.

Using the definition of miracle that we learned, is the author of the Hallel describing a miracle?

(yes)

What's the miracle?

(the Exodus itself)

How do you know?

(from the choice of words used to describe the event)

What kinds of words are they?

(they are poetic; they are metaphors)

So both these texts talk about the Exodus. Both may even understand the Exodus as a miracle. But both have very different feeling tones or moods.

What's interesting is that the manner in which these texts are recited in the synagogue reflects the moods and feelings that we have been discussing. When we recite Birkat Geulah in the Maariv service, we are seated. The text may be said silently or responsively. Sometimes a portion of it may be sung. As we say the words, we think about the Exodus; we contemplate its wondrousness.

The Hallel, on the other hand, is recited while standing. There is a lot of communal singing and responsive singing. The standing and the community singing enhance the feeling of joyfulness, celebration and wonder that the words themselves express. Here the feeling overwhelms the person reciting the words. It is not a time for contemplation, but for entering into the wondrous feelings that the words express.

The obvious next step is to teach students to read this paragraph accurately and to chant it in the way in which it is chanted in your local synagogue.

Closing

Imagine you had been with the Israelites leaving Egypt.

What do you think it must have been like? How did it look? How did it feel?

Take a few minutes to think about these questions and then try to capture these feelings, these emotions in either a paragraph or poem or a drawing.

When students have finished, hang up their work on the walls of the classroom and ask all students to walk around and examine each others work. This technique of sharing can be compared to a museum visit where you walk around and look at the works others have created. You may want to ask students also to share their responses orally.

Text for Students

We affirm the truth that He is our God, that there is no other, and that we are His people Israel. He redeems us from the power of kings, delivers us from the hand of all tyrants. He brings judgment upon our oppressors, retribution upon all our mortal enemies. He performs wonders beyond understanding, marvels beyond all reckoning. He has maintained us among the living. He has not allowed our steps to falter. He guided us to triumph over mighty foes, exalted our strength over all our enemies. He vindicated us with miracles before Pharaoh, with signs and wonders in the land of Egypt. In wrath He smote all of Egypt's firstborn, bringing His people to lasting freedom. He led His children through divided waters as their pursuers sank in the sea.

When His children beheld His might they sang in praise of Him, gladly accepting His sovereignty. Moses and the people Israel sang with great joy to the Lord:

Mi khamokha ba-eilim Adonai, mi kamokha, nedar ba-kodesh, nora t'hilot, oseh feleh.

Who is like You, Lord, among all that is worshiped? Who is like You, majestic in holiness, awesome in splendor, working wonders?

Your children beheld Your sovereignty as You divided the sea before Moses. "This is my God," they responded, declaring:

Adonai yimlokh l'olam va-ed.

"The Lord shall reign throughout all time."

And thus it is written: "The Lord has rescued Jacob; He redeemed him from those more powerful." Praised are You, Lord, Redeemer of the people Israel.

Hebrew text and English translation from <u>Siddur Sim Shalom</u> edited by Rabbi Jules Harlow (New York: The Rabbinical Assembly, 1985)

Text for Students

אֱמֶת וֶאֱמוּנָה כָּל־זֹאת וְקַיָּם עָלֵינוּ, כִּי הוּא יהוה אֱלֹהֵינוּ וְאֵין
זוּלָתוֹ, וַאֲנַחְנוּ יִשְׂרָאֵל עַמּוֹ. הַפּוֹדֵנוּ מִיַּד מְלָכִים, מַלְכֵּנוּ
הַגּוֹאֲלֵנוּ מִכַּף כָּל־הֶעָרִיצִים, הָאֵל הַנִּפְרָע לָנוּ מִצָּרֵינוּ
וְהַמְשַׁלֵּם גְּמוּל לְכָל־אֹיְבֵי נַפְשֵׁנוּ, הָעוֹשֶׂה גְדוֹלוֹת עַד אֵין
חֵקֶר וְנִפְלָאוֹת עַד אֵין מִסְפָּר, הַשָּׂם נַפְשֵׁנוּ בַּחַיִּים וְלֹא נָתַן
לַמּוֹט רַגְלֵנוּ, הַמַּדְרִיכֵנוּ עַל בָּמוֹת אוֹיְבֵינוּ וַיָּרֶם קַרְנֵנוּ עַל כָּל־
שׂוֹנְאֵינוּ, הָעוֹשֶׂה לָנוּ נִסִּים וּנְקָמָה בְּפַרְעֹה, אוֹתוֹת וּמוֹפְתִים
בְּאַדְמַת בְּנֵי חָם, הַמַּכֶּה בְעֶבְרָתוֹ כָּל־בְּכוֹרֵי מִצְרָיִם, וַיּוֹצֵא
אֶת־עַמּוֹ יִשְׂרָאֵל מִתּוֹכָם לְחֵרוּת עוֹלָם, הַמַּעֲבִיר בָּנָיו בֵּין גִּזְרֵי
יַם סוּף, אֶת־רוֹדְפֵיהֶם וְאֶת־שׂוֹנְאֵיהֶם בִּתְהוֹמוֹת טִבַּע, וְרָאוּ
בָנָיו גְבוּרָתוֹ, שִׁבְּחוּ וְהוֹדוּ לִשְׁמוֹ. ☐ וּמַלְכוּתוֹ בְּרָצוֹן קִבְּלוּ
עֲלֵיהֶם. מֹשֶׁה וּבְנֵי יִשְׂרָאֵל לְךָ עָנוּ שִׁירָה בְּשִׂמְחָה רַבָּה,
וְאָמְרוּ כֻלָּם:
מִי כָמֹכָה בָּאֵלִם יהוה, מִי כָּמֹכָה נֶאְדָּר בַּקֹּדֶשׁ, נוֹרָא תְהִלֹּת
עֹשֵׂה פֶלֶא.

☐ מַלְכוּתְךָ רָאוּ בָנֶיךָ, בּוֹקֵעַ יָם לִפְנֵי מֹשֶׁה, זֶה אֵלִי עָנוּ
וְאָמְרוּ: יהוה יִמְלֹךְ לְעֹלָם וָעֶד.

☐ וְנֶאֱמַר: כִּי פָדָה יהוה אֶת־יַעֲקֹב, וּגְאָלוֹ מִיַּד חָזָק מִמֶּנּוּ.
בָּרוּךְ אַתָּה יהוה גָּאַל יִשְׂרָאֵל.

Hebrew text and English translation from <u>Siddur Sim Shalom</u> edited by Rabbi Jules Harlow (New York: The Rabbinical Assembly, 1985)

85

Text for Students

בְּצֵאת יִשְׂרָאֵל מִמִּצְרָיִם, בֵּית יַעֲקֹב מֵעַם לֹעֵז.

הָיְתָה יְהוּדָה לְקָדְשׁוֹ, יִשְׂרָאֵל מַמְשְׁלוֹתָיו.

הַיָּם רָאָה וַיָּנֹס, הַיַּרְדֵּן יִסֹּב לְאָחוֹר.

הֶהָרִים רָקְדוּ כְאֵילִים, גְּבָעוֹת כִּבְנֵי צֹאן.

מַה לְּךָ הַיָּם כִּי תָנוּס, הַיַּרְדֵּן תִּסֹּב לְאָחוֹר.

הֶהָרִים תִּרְקְדוּ כְאֵילִים, גְּבָעוֹת כִּבְנֵי־צֹאן.

□ מִלְּפְנֵי אָדוֹן חוּלִי אָרֶץ, מִלִּפְנֵי אֱלוֹהַּ יַעֲקֹב,

הַהֹפְכִי הַצּוּר אֲגַם מָיִם, חַלָּמִישׁ לְמַעְיְנוֹ מָיִם.

When Israel left the land of Egypt,
when the House of Jacob left alien people,

Judah became His holy one; Israel, His domain.

The sea fled at the sight; the Jordan retreated.

Mountains leaped like rams; and hills, like lambs.

O sea, why did you flee? Jordan, why did you retreat?

Mountains, why leap like rams; and hills, like lambs?

Even the earth trembled at the Lord's Presence,
at the Presence of Jacob's God.

He turns rock into pools of water; flint, into fountains.

PSALM 114

Hebrew text and English translation from <u>Siddur Sim Shalom</u> edited by Rabbi Jules Harlow (New York: The Rabbinical Assembly, 1985)

YOM HA'ATZMA'UT

Overview

In this lesson, students think about how holidays become holidays. They study two kinds of Jewish holidays--those which reflect early experiences in the life of the Jewish people and are already written into the text of the Torah and those which come into being later as the result of the experiences of the Jewish people throughout the ages. Purim and Yom Ha'Atzma'ut are used as examples of this second kind of holiday.

In this lesson, students learn that holidays are not just times set aside to mark special events of the distant past. In every generation, people experience events that can potentially become holidays. What makes an event a holiday in the Jewish tradition is: the Jewish people's interpretation of the event as an experience of the presence of God and the subsequent creation of liturgical expressions which mark the experience.

The lesson begins by asking students to list American holidays, their origins, and the ways in which they are celebrated.

Students then turn to the question of Jewish holidays. They study two Torah texts (Deuteronomy 16, and Numbers 28 and 29) in order to find out which of the Jewish holidays are already mentioned in the Torah text.

Students notice that not all the holidays we celebrate are mentioned in the Torah text, e.g., Purim and Hanukkah. They next study a selection from Megillat Esther (chapter 9) and find out how Purim came into being. They compare the ways in which we celebrate Purim today and the ways that the text of Megillat Esther suggest celebrating Purim. They discover that certain Purim celebrations have their origin in the Megillah and others don't. They speculate that these later observances (those not written about in the Megillah) were created to help those of us who did not actually experience the "miracle" of Purim understand the holiday better.

They then study the evolution of Yom Ha'atzma'ut and create a list which suggests the stages of development of a Jewish holiday.

Optional closing activity asks students to think how they might "institutionalize" the celebration of either יוֹם יְרוּשָׁלַיִם or יוֹם הַשׁוֹאָה.

Materials: JPS Torah translation or photocopy of Deuteronomy 16 and Numbers 28 and 29. Megillat Esther, Chapter 9. Photocopy texts of עַל הַנִּסִּים for Hanukkah, Purim, Yom Ha'atzma'ut are found at the end of the lesson.

Setting The Stage

<u>Name some American holidays. Tell what they celebrate or commemorate.</u>

You might want to list the holidays on the board so that students can refer back to them as they answer the questions that follow. List might include holidays such as Thanksgiving, Fourth of July, George Washington's Birthday, Martin Luther King's Birthday, etc.

<u>How did these holidays come into being?</u>

(popular sentiment, people created them, laws of Congress)

<u>Look back over this list. Choose a holiday and tell me how it is celebrated.</u>

<u>Does anyone know how this particular holiday came to be celebrated in the way that it is?</u>

Lesson

In this lesson, we're going to think about Jewish holidays, their origins and how we have come to celebrate them. Let's begin by creating a list of Jewish holidays.

List holidays on the board. Try to get a pretty complete list.

<u>Let's find out how these holidays came into being.</u>

<u>If students have the skills and you have access to JPS Torah or the synagogue's H.umash, ask them to find the actual sources in the text. If this is not possible, xerox copies of the texts found at the end of the unit.</u>

<u>First let's look at chapter 16 of Deuteronomy.</u>

Read it.

<u>What holidays are mentioned there?</u>

You may ask students to do this reading in small groups. Or you may want to do this as a whole group lesson, asking students to take turns reading while others listen.

Or you may want to read the text aloud, asking students to stop you each time they hear you mention the name of a holiday.

(The list of holidays on the board should include:

פֶּסַח, vv. 1-8

שָׁבֻעוֹת--Feast of Weeks, vv. 9-12

סֻכּוֹת--Feast of Booths, vv. 13-15)

At this point, examine the list of Jewish holidays already on the board. Check off the holidays mentioned in Chapter 16 of Deuteronomy. And say something like:

> Well, now we know that three of the holidays that we listed already existed by the time the Torah was written down. (By the time of the destruction of the Second Temple in 70 A.D.)

> Let's look at one other place in the Torah which lists holidays, Numbers or בְּמִדְבַּר, chapters 28 and 29. This list is more extensive. Let's read it and find out what holidays it mentions.

Again choose the method of reading that suits your group, listing the holidays as you read. Because some of the holidays are mentioned by day and month and not by name, students may need more help figuring out to which holidays the text refers. When students have completed the reading, again compare the list of holidays in the text with the list on the board.

The following list includes the holidays in the text. There are two names listed when the text uses a name that students may not recognize. The name on the left is the name used in the text. The name on the right is the name students have learned for the holiday.

Chapter 28

שַׁבָּת, *vv. 9-10*

New Moon--רֹאשׁ חֹדֶשׁ, *vv. 11-15*

פֶּסַח, *vv. 16-25*

Feast of Weeks--שָׁבֻעוֹת, *vv. 26-31*

Chapter 29

רֹאשׁ הַשָּׁנָה, *vv. 1-6*

יוֹם כִּפּוּר, *vv. 7-11*

סֻכּוֹת, *vv. 12-38*

What additional holidays are mentioned in these two chapters?

(יוֹם כִּפּוּר, רֹאשׁ הַשָּׁנָה, רֹאשׁ חֹדֶשׁ, שַׁבָּת)

Now look back again at the list of Jewish holidays on the board.

This time check off those holidays which students referred to that are mentioned in the Torah. Add any holidays that they left off their list.

As we are looking at our lists, you can see that we have mentioned holidays that are not mentioned in these two Torah selections. Which holidays are they?

(Most lists will probably include: חֲנֻכָּה, פּוּרִים; maybe, ט"וּ בִּשְׁבָט and יוֹם הָעַצְמָאוּת)

Why do you think they aren't mentioned?

(Maybe they came into being after the Torah was written)

That's right. We have mentioned holidays that came into being after the time that the Torah was written. An example of a holiday that is on our list whose origin you can find in the Bible, but not in the Torah is Purim.

At this point, hand out copies of Megillat Esther, chapter 9. This text can probably be read by individuals in order to vary the pace of the lesson.

I'd like each of you to read this text. It's from Megillat Esther. Find the verses that tell you how Purim became a holiday and underline them.

(vv. 20-23)

What do these verses tell you about how Purim came into being?

(The people who lived during the time that these events took place decided to celebrate/commemorate what happened to them by creating a holiday.)

How did they make it into a holiday? How did they suggest that the day be observed?

List the answers on the board. They can be found in verse 22.

(feasting, merrymaking, an occasion for sending gifts to one another, presents to the poor)

Are these the only ways in which we celebrate Purim?(no)

I can think of one very central observance that is not on this list. What is it?

(reading the Megillah)

<u>Why do you think that it doesn't appear on the list of observances mentioned in מְגִלַּת אֶסְתֵּר?</u>

(There was no Megillah yet. The events had just happened.)

<u>Why do you think the custom of reading the Megillah came into being?</u>

(For later generations who had not experienced the event just feasting and sending gifts was not enough. They needed to retell the story in order to have a reason to celebrate.)

I think that's right. Generations who came later, people who had not experienced the events of the story needed more rituals, more formal reminders to help them celebrate Purim and feel its power and importance. In fact, later generations not only added a Megillah reading to the Arvit and Shaharit services, they also added a Torah reading during Shaharit and a version of עַל הַנִּסִּים written especially for Purim. All of these customs have become part of how we celebrate the holiday today.

<u>Looking at the board, what other holidays are mentioned that began after the Torah was written?</u>

(Hanukkah is such a holiday, and if Yom Ha'atzma'ut is on the board, it is also such a holiday.)

Hanukkah is another example of a holiday where we read about a special event happening in the life of the Jewish people. People living at the time experienced the event as a miracle. They established a holiday. We studied this at Hanukkah time where we looked at the text of עַל הַנִּסִּים.

So far, all the holidays that we have studied began a really long time ago. However, we are living at a special time in the history of the Jewish people, because we are watching and participating in the creation of a holiday. The holiday I'm thinking about is Yom Ha'atzma'ut.

<u>First of all, who can tell us what Yom Ha'atzma'ut is?</u>

(Israel's Independence Day)

<u>In what year did the state of Israel become an independent state?</u>

(1948)

<u>So is Yom Ha'atzma'ut a holiday that we can learn about from the Torah?</u>

(no)

Of course not. Yom Ha'atzma'ut is a holiday like Purim and Hanukkah. It is a holiday created by people who have lived through an exceptional event and understood the event as a reflection of the presence of God.

<u>What is the exceptional event in this case?</u>

(the founding of the independent state of Israel)

<u>How do we usually celebrate Yom Ha'atzma'ut?</u>

(Usually we have some kind of school assembly, we may eat felafel)

In Israel, to begin with, Yom Ha'atzma'ut was celebrated a lot like we celebrate our Independence Day. How do we celebrate the Fourth of July?

(picnics, parades, family outings)

But as you already realize that's not how we generally celebrate other Jewish holidays.

If you look at our list of holidays, what observances do most of them have in common?

(some kind of family get together involving food, some kind of synagogue celebration)

Yom Ha'atzma'ut is now becoming a holiday with more of the regular features of other Jewish holidays that we have talked about.

Based on that information, what do you think is being added to the picnics and parades that are already part of the Yom Ha'atzma'ut celebration?

(some kind of synagogue component)

Right you are. There is now a Torah reading for Yom Ha'atzma'ut (Deuteronomy 7:12-8:18), a Haftarah reading (Isaiah 10:32-12:6). We also say Hallel and an עַל הַנִּסִּים composed especially for Yom Ha'atzma'ut.

To get more of a first hand sense of this process of the making of a Jewish holiday, I'd like you to read the Yom Ha'atzma'ut version of the עַל הַנִּסִּים and compare it to the versions of the עַל הַנִּסִּים for Hanukkah and Purim.

These texts can be found in <u>Siddur Sim Shalom</u> on pages 180-183. Copies of these texts can also be found at the end of this lesson and can be xeroxed for students' use.

This assignment may be done in small groups. Ask them to look for things about these texts that are similar and things that are different.

(Probable answers include: the opening lines are the same; in the עַל הַנִּסִּים of Hanukkah and Yom Ha'atzma'ut, the closing lines are also the same; each one describes a specific event different from the others; each describes a military victory)

All of these answers are correct. An interesting feature of all these texts is that in each one a nationalistic, military event that could have been described only in terms of being a military victory is interpreted as a religious event. The selection that we read from Martin Buber when we studied about Hanukkah can help us here. These three holidays are all based on people experiencing an extraordinary event in their lives as a miracle and commemorating it. The written prayers are one example of this commemoration. The writing of a prayer is a way for one generation to share their feelings about an event that happened to them with other generations of Jews for whom the event was not a first hand experience.

Closing

Today, we've been talking about the making of a Jewish holiday. Using Purim or Yom Ha'atzma'ut as examples, let's recreate the steps from "no holiday" to Jewish holiday.

You may want to list these steps on the board.

> 1. event that calls for commemoration
>
> 2. celebration of the event with certain informal joyfulness and outreach to family and friends
>
> 3. full fledged holiday with customs and ceremonies of its own usually including additions to synagogue service, like reading from Torah and some kind of prayer that marks the occasion.

Optional: You might want to ask students to speculate about a day like יוֹם הַשׁוֹאָה or יוֹם יְרוּשָׁלַיִם --days which also commemorate events that we as a people want to remember, but which have not yet been made into Jewish holidays as we have defined them. What might they suggest as forms and customs that could be added to either to enhance their "holidayness."

Alternatively, you might want to end by asking students to think a little more about Yom Ha'atzma'ut and what else might be added to it to enhance its "holidayness."

Texts for Students

On Purim:

We thank You for the heroism, for the triumphs, and for the miraculous deliverance of our ancestors, in other days and in our time.

In the days of Mordecai and Esther, in Shushan, the capital of Persia, the wicked Haman rose up against all Jews and plotted their destruction. In a single day, the thirteenth of Adar, the twelfth month of the year, Haman planned to annihilate all Jews, young and old, and to permit the plunder of their property. You, in great mercy, thwarted his designs, frustrated his plot, and visited upon him the evil he planned to bring on others. Haman, together with his sons, suffered death on the gallows he had made for Mordecai.

On Israel's Independence Day:

We thank You for the heroism, for the triumphs, and for the miraculous deliverance of our ancestors, in other days and in our time.

In the days when Your children were returning to their borders, at the time of a people revived in its land as in days of old, the gates to the land of our ancestors were closed before those who were fleeing the sword. When enemies from within the land together with seven neighboring nations sought to annihilate Your people, You, in Your great mercy, stood by them in time of trouble. You defended them and vindicated them. You gave them the courage to meet their foes, to open the gates to those seeking refuge, and to free the land of its armed invaders. You delivered the many into the hands of the few, the guilty into the hands of the innocent. You have wrought great victories and miraculous deliverance for Your people Israel to this day, revealing Your glory and Your holiness to all the world.

For all these blessings we shall ever praise and exalt You.

Hebrew text from Siddur Sim Shalom edited by Rabbi Jules Harlow (New York: The Rabbinical Assembly, 1985)

Texts for Students

On Purim:

עַל הַנִּסִּים וְעַל הַפֻּרְקָן, וְעַל הַגְּבוּרוֹת, וְעַל הַתְּשׁוּעוֹת, וְעַל הַמִּלְחָמוֹת שֶׁעָשִׂיתָ לַאֲבוֹתֵינוּ בַּיָּמִים הָהֵם וּבַזְּמַן הַזֶּה.

בִּימֵי מָרְדְּכַי וְאֶסְתֵּר בְּשׁוּשַׁן הַבִּירָה, כְּשֶׁעָמַד עֲלֵיהֶם הָמָן הָרָשָׁע, בִּקֵּשׁ לְהַשְׁמִיד לַהֲרוֹג וּלְאַבֵּד אֶת־כָּל־הַיְּהוּדִים, מִנַּעַר וְעַד זָקֵן, טַף וְנָשִׁים, בְּיוֹם אֶחָד, בִּשְׁלוֹשָׁה עָשָׂר לְחֹדֶשׁ שְׁנֵים־עָשָׂר, הוּא חֹדֶשׁ אֲדָר, וּשְׁלָלָם לָבוֹז. וְאַתָּה בְּרַחֲמֶיךָ הָרַבִּים הֵפַרְתָּ אֶת־עֲצָתוֹ, וְקִלְקַלְתָּ אֶת־מַחֲשַׁבְתּוֹ, וַהֲשֵׁבוֹתָ גְּמוּלוֹ בְּרֹאשׁוֹ, וְתָלוּ אוֹתוֹ וְאֶת־בָּנָיו עַל הָעֵץ.

On Israel's Independence Day:

עַל הַנִּסִּים וְעַל הַפֻּרְקָן, וְעַל הַגְּבוּרוֹת, וְעַל הַתְּשׁוּעוֹת, וְעַל הַמִּלְחָמוֹת שֶׁעָשִׂיתָ לַאֲבוֹתֵינוּ בַּיָּמִים הָהֵם וּבַזְּמַן הַזֶּה.

בִּימֵי שִׁיבַת בָּנִים לִגְבוּלָם, בְּעֵת תְּקוּמַת עַם בְּאַרְצוֹ כִּימֵי קֶדֶם, נִסְגְּרוּ שַׁעֲרֵי אֶרֶץ אָבוֹת בִּפְנֵי אַחֵינוּ פְּלִיטֵי חֶרֶב, וְאוֹיְבִים בָּאָרֶץ וְשִׁבְעָה עֲמָמִים בַּעֲלֵי בְּרִיתָם קָמוּ לְהַכְרִית עַמְּךָ יִשְׂרָאֵל, וְאַתָּה בְּרַחֲמֶיךָ הָרַבִּים עָמַדְתָּ לָהֶם בְּעֵת צָרָתָם, רַבְתָּ אֶת־רִיבָם, דַּנְתָּ אֶת־דִּינָם, חִזַּקְתָּ אֶת־לִבָּם לַעֲמוֹד בַּשַּׁעַר, וְלִפְתֹּחַ שְׁעָרִים לַנִּרְדָּפִים וּלְגָרֵשׁ אֶת־צִבְאוֹת הָאוֹיֵב מִן הָאָרֶץ. מָסַרְתָּ רַבִּים בְּיַד מְעַטִּים, וּרְשָׁעִים בְּיַד צַדִּיקִים, וּלְךָ עָשִׂיתָ שֵׁם גָּדוֹל וְקָדוֹשׁ בְּעוֹלָמֶךָ, וּלְעַמְּךָ יִשְׂרָאֵל עָשִׂיתָ תְּשׁוּעָה גְדוֹלָה וּפֻרְקָן כְּהַיּוֹם הַזֶּה.

וְעַל כֻּלָּם יִתְבָּרַךְ וְיִתְרוֹמַם שִׁמְךָ מַלְכֵּנוּ תָּמִיד לְעוֹלָם וָעֶד.

Hebrew text from <u>Siddur Sim Shalom</u> edited by Rabbi Jules Harlow (New York: The Rabbinical Assembly, 1985)

Texts for Students

On Ḥanukkah:

We thank You for the heroism, for the triumphs, and for the miraculous deliverance of our ancestors, in other days and in our time.

In the days of Mattathias son of Yoḥanan, the Hasmonean *kohen gadol*, and in the days of his sons, a cruel power rose against Israel, demanding that they abandon Your Torah and violate Your mitzvot. You, in great mercy, stood by Your people in time of trouble. You defended them, vindicated them, and avenged their wrongs. You delivered the strong into the hands of the pure in heart, the guilty into the hands of the innocent. You delivered the arrogant into the hands of those who were faithful to Your Torah. You have wrought great victories and miraculous deliverance for Your people Israel to this day, revealing Your glory and Your holiness to all the world. Then Your children came into Your shrine, cleansed Your Temple, purified Your sanctuary, and kindled lights in Your sacred courts. They set aside these eight days as a season for giving thanks and reciting praises to You.

Hebrew text from Siddur Sim Shalom edited by Rabbi Jules Harlow (New York: The Rabbinical Assembly, 1985)

Texts for Students

On Ḥanukkah:

עַל הַנִּסִּים וְעַל הַפֻּרְקָן, וְעַל הַגְּבוּרוֹת, וְעַל הַתְּשׁוּעוֹת, וְעַל
הַמִּלְחָמוֹת שֶׁעָשִׂיתָ לַאֲבוֹתֵינוּ בַּיָּמִים הָהֵם וּבַזְּמַן הַזֶּה.

בִּימֵי מַתִּתְיָהוּ בֶּן־יוֹחָנָן כֹּהֵן גָּדוֹל, חַשְׁמוֹנַי וּבָנָיו, כְּשֶׁעָמְדָה
מַלְכוּת יָוָן הָרְשָׁעָה עַל עַמְּךָ יִשְׂרָאֵל לְהַשְׁכִּיחָם תּוֹרָתֶךָ וּלְהַעֲבִירָם
מֵחֻקֵּי רְצוֹנֶךָ, וְאַתָּה בְּרַחֲמֶיךָ הָרַבִּים עָמַדְתָּ לָהֶם בְּעֵת צָרָתָם,
רַבְתָּ אֶת־רִיבָם, דַּנְתָּ אֶת־דִּינָם, נָקַמְתָּ אֶת־נִקְמָתָם, מָסַרְתָּ גִבּוֹרִים
בְּיַד חַלָּשִׁים, וְרַבִּים בְּיַד מְעַטִּים, וּטְמֵאִים בְּיַד טְהוֹרִים, וּרְשָׁעִים
בְּיַד צַדִּיקִים, וְזֵדִים בְּיַד עוֹסְקֵי תוֹרָתֶךָ. וּלְךָ עָשִׂיתָ שֵׁם גָּדוֹל
וְקָדוֹשׁ בְּעוֹלָמֶךָ, וּלְעַמְּךָ יִשְׂרָאֵל עָשִׂיתָ תְּשׁוּעָה גְדוֹלָה וּפֻרְקָן
כְּהַיּוֹם הַזֶּה. וְאַחַר כֵּן בָּאוּ בָנֶיךָ לִדְבִיר בֵּיתֶךָ וּפִנּוּ אֶת־הֵיכָלֶךָ,
וְטִהֲרוּ אֶת־מִקְדָּשֶׁךָ, וְהִדְלִיקוּ נֵרוֹת בְּחַצְרוֹת קָדְשֶׁךָ, וְקָבְעוּ
שְׁמוֹנַת יְמֵי חֲנֻכָּה אֵלּוּ לְהוֹדוֹת וּלְהַלֵּל לְשִׁמְךָ הַגָּדוֹל.

Hebrew text from <u>Siddur Sim Shalom</u> edited by Rabbi Jules Harlow (New York: The Rabbinical Assembly, 1985)

9 And so, on the thirteenth day of the twelfth month—that is, the month of Adar—when the king's command and decree were to be executed, the very day on which the enemies of the Jews had expected to get them in their power, the opposite happened, and the Jews got their enemies in their power. [2] Throughout the provinces of King Ahasuerus, the Jews mustered in their cities to attack those who sought their hurt; and no one could withstand them, for the fear of them had fallen upon all the peoples. [3] Indeed, all the officials of the provinces—the satraps, the governors, and the king's stewards—showed deference to the Jews, because the fear of Mordecai had fallen upon them. [4] For Mordecai was now powerful in the royal palace, and his fame was spreading through all the provinces; the man Mordecai was growing ever more powerful. [5] So the Jews struck at their enemies with the sword, slaying and destroying; they wreaked their will upon their enemies.

[6] In the fortress Shushan the Jews killed a total of five hundred men. [7] They also killed[a] Parshandatha, Dalphon, Aspatha, [8] Poratha, Adalia, Aridatha, [9] Parmashta, Arisai, Aridai, and Vaizatha, [10] the ten sons of Haman son of Hammedatha, the foe of the Jews. But they did not lay hands on the spoil. [11] When the number of those slain in the fortress Shushan was reported on that same day to the king, [12] the king said to Queen Esther, "In the fortress Shushan alone the Jews have killed a total of five hundred men, as well as the ten sons of Haman. What then must they have done in the provinces of the realm! What is your wish now? It shall be granted you. And what else is your request? It shall be fulfilled." [13] "If it please Your Majesty," Esther replied, "let the Jews in Shushan be permitted to act tomorrow also as they did today; and let Haman's ten sons be impaled on the stake." [14] The king ordered that this should be done, and the decree was proclaimed in Shushan. Haman's ten sons were impaled: [15] and the Jews in Shushan mustered again on the fourteenth day of Adar and slew three hundred men in Shushan. But they did not lay hands on the spoil.

[16] The rest of the Jews, those in the king's provinces, likewise mustered and fought for their lives. They disposed of their enemies, killing seventy-five thousand of their foes; but they did not lay hands on the spoil. [17] That was on the thirteenth day of the month of Adar; and they rested on the fourteenth day and made it a day of feasting and merrymaking. ([18] But the Jews in Shushan mustered on both the thirteenth and fourteenth days, and so rested on the fifteenth, and made it a day of feasting and merrymaking.) [19] That is why village Jews, who live in unwalled

towns, observe the fourteenth day of the month of Adar and make it a day of merrymaking and feasting, and as a holiday and an occasion for sending gifts to one another.

20 Mordecai recorded these events. And he sent dispatches to all the Jews throughout the provinces of King Ahasuerus, near and far, 21 charging them to observe the fourteenth and fifteenth days of Adar, every year—22 the same days on which the Jews enjoyed relief from their foes and the same month which had been transformed for them from one of grief and mourning to one of festive joy. They were to observe them as days of feasting and merrymaking, and as an occasion for sending gifts to one another and presents to the poor. 23 The Jews accordingly assumed as an obligation that which they had begun to practice and which Mordecai prescribed for them.

24 For Haman son of Hammedatha the Agagite, the foe of all the Jews, had plotted to destroy the Jews, and had cast *pur*—that is, the lot—with intent to crush and exterminate them. 25 But when [Esther] came before the king, he commanded: *b*"With the promulgation of this decree,*-b* let the evil plot, which he devised against the Jews, recoil on his own head!" So they impaled him and his sons on the stake. 26 For that reason these days were named Purim, after *pur*.

In view, then, of all the instructions in the said letter and of what they had experienced in that matter and what had befallen them, 27 the Jews undertook and irrevocably obligated themselves and their descendants, and all who might join them, to observe these two days in the manner prescribed and at the proper time each year. 28 Consequently, these days are recalled and observed in every generation: by every family, every province, and every city. And these days of Purim shall never cease among the Jews, and the memory of them shall never perish among their descendants.

29 *c*Then Queen Esther daughter of Abihail wrote a second letter of Purim for the purpose of confirming with full authority the aforementioned one of Mordecai the Jew. 30 Dispatches were sent to all the Jews in the hundred and twenty-seven provinces of the realm of Ahasuerus with an ordinance of "equity and honesty*d*": 31 These days of Purim shall be observed at their proper time, as Mordecai the Jew—and now Queen Esther—has obligated them to do, and just as they have assumed for themselves and their descendants the obligation of the fasts with their lamentations.*e*

32 And Esther's ordinance validating these observances of Purim was recorded in a scroll.

(from <u>The Tanakh</u>: Jewish Publication Society translation of the Bible)

SHAVUOT

Overview

This is the last of the tefillah lessons in the dalet year. The question students are asked to address is: what is the source of the קְדֻשָּׁה, holiness or specialness, of any holiday. In order to answer this question, they will examine the חֲתִימָה of the קְדֻשַׁת הַיּוֹם section of each holiday's Amidah as well as the text of the וַיְכֻלּוּ. These texts suggest that God is the source of a holiday's holiness.

Students are then asked to analyze their own holiday experiences as well as the midrashic tale "The Sabbath Taste" by Sadie Rose Weilerstein. These sources seem to support the notion that a holiday's holiness comes from the energy and efforts of people.

Students and teacher discuss this paradox. The goal of the lesson is to help students understand the role that each individual plays in perpetuating Jewish tradition—represented here in a discussion of holidays.

As students approach their Bar/ Bat mitzvah year, it becomes critical that they understand that they are the next link in the chain of Jewish tradition and that they have choices. In terms of holiday celebrations, if they choose to opt out, then the holidays, as we know them, will cease to exist. We may have a memory of days set aside by the tradition, but without ongoing involvement these days will not remain holidays. They will disappear.

Materials: photocopies of "The Sabbath Taste" and of וַיְכֻלּוּ, both attached at the end of the lesson.

Setting the Stage

Write the following berakhot on the board or on an acetate for use with an overhead projector.

בָּרוּךְ אַתָּה ה׳ מְקַדֵּשׁ הַשַּׁבָּת

בָּרוּךְ אַתָּה ה׳ מְקַדֵּשׁ יִשְׂרָאֵל וְיוֹם הַזִּכָּרוֹן

101

בָּרוּךְ אַתָּה ה' מְקַדֵּשׁ יִשְׂרָאֵל וְיוֹם הַכִּפֻּרִים

בָּרוּךְ אַתָּה ה' מְקַדֵּשׁ יִשְׂרָאֵל וְרָאשֵׁי חֳדָשִׁים

בָּרוּךְ אַתָּה ה' מְקַדֵּשׁ יִשְׂרָאֵל וְהַזְּמַנִּים

Begin the lesson by calling on volunteers to read the berakhot on the board.

<u>What do all these berakhot have in common?</u>

(Possible answers include: ה' אַתָּה בָּרוּךְ, מְקַדֵּשׁ, מְקַדֵּשׁ יִשְׂרָאֵל (for all except Shabbat)

Lesson

<u>This year, we've been relating our study of the Siddur to the holidays. All of the verses on the board come from the holiday tefillot. Does anyone want to guess where we would find them?</u>

Whether or not students guess, you can continue by saying something like:

You are looking at the concluding line of the middle section of each holiday Amidah.

You probably all remember very well the structure of the Amidah. On weekdays, חוֹל, the Amidah has three introductory berakhot: גְּבוּרוֹת, אָבוֹת, קְדֻשַׁת ה', and three concluding berakhot: עֲבוֹדָה, הוֹדָאָה and בִּרְכַּת הַשָּׁלוֹם, and thirteen middle berakhot of petition or request called בַּקָּשׁוֹת.

You may want to chart them on the board as a review.

<u>חַג</u>	<u>חוֹל</u>
אָבוֹת	אָבוֹת
גְּבוּרוֹת	גְּבוּרוֹת
קְדֻשַׁת ה'	קְדֻשַׁת ה'
קְדֻשַׁת הַיּוֹם	בַּקָּשׁוֹת (13)
עֲבוֹדָה	עֲבוֹדָה
הוֹדָאָה	הוֹדָאָה
בִּרְכַּת הַשָּׁלוֹם	בִּרְכַּת הַשָּׁלוֹם

On Shabbat and holidays, the section of בַּקָּשׁוֹת does not appear in the Amidah. You probably remember this from our Shabbat lessons this year. On each and every holiday the same thing holds true: the middle section is replaced with a section which talks about the specialness of the holiday. That berakha is always called קְדֻשַּׁת הַיּוֹם.

If you have made a chart, insert the קְדֻשַּׁת הַיּוֹם *on the opposite side of the board. And either rewrite the 3 introductory or concluding berakhot or indicate that they are the same by drawing arrows across the board.*

On the board, I have written the concluding lines of the berakhot "קְדֻשַּׁת הַיּוֹם" for each special holiday Amidah. For some of these berakhot the holiday it refers to is clear; for others it's not. Let's look at these חֲתִימוֹת again. As each volunteer reads, I'd like the reader to tell us which holiday they think the berakha refers to.

Ask for volunteers to read.

Shabbat : בָּרוּךְ אַתָּה ה׳ מְקַדֵּשׁ הַשַּׁבָּת

Rosh Hashanah : בָּרוּךְ אַתָּה ה׳ מְקַדֵּשׁ יִשְׂרָאֵל וְיוֹם הַזִּכָּרוֹן

Yom Kippur : בָּרוּךְ אַתָּה ה׳ מְקַדֵּשׁ יִשְׂרָאֵל וְיוֹם הַכִּפֻּרִים

Rosh Hodesh : בָּרוּךְ אַתָּה ה׳ מְקַדֵּשׁ יִשְׂרָאֵל וְרָאשֵׁי חֳדָשִׁים

Pesah, Shavuot, and Sukkot : בָּרוּךְ אַתָּה ה׳ מְקַדֵּשׁ יִשְׂרָאֵל וְהַזְּמַנִּים

There are 2 elements that all of these verses have in common. You have mentioned them already. The first is that they are berakhot. They begin with the words: בָּרוּךְ אַתָּה ה׳.

The second is they all refer to God as מְקַדֵּשׁ—the Sanctifier, the One who makes holy or special.

The verb קָדַשׁ in Hebrew means holy, or separate or set apart, different, unique. Using this translation of the verb, we might say God sets apart these times as holiday times. If you take a close look at the English word "holiday," you can see that this idea of holy day is also there. A holy day—a day set apart.

Perhaps write "holy day—holiday" on board.

<u>Where do you think that the idea that God is the source of the holiness or separateness of these days comes from?</u> (allow students to speculate)

One source is the Bible. In the very beginning of the Torah, in the book of Genesis, we read the section that I'm handing out to you. Underline in English and in Hebrew the words or phrases that describe how Shabbat got to be so special.

The וַיְכֻלּוּ is attached at the end of this lesson.

<u>Do you remember where we find the וַיְכֻלּוּ in the siddur?</u>

(Friday evening קִדּוּשׁ and the קְדֻשַּׁת הַיּוֹם for Friday night.

<u>Which were the words or phrases that you underlined that describe how Shabbat got to be so special.</u>

(וַיְבָרֶךְ אֱלֹהִים אֶת יוֹם הַשְּׁבִיעִי וַיְקַדֵּשׁ אֹתוֹ)

(God blessed the 7th day and set it apart, made it holy.)

<u>But let me ask you a question. From your understanding is that how it works? Think about Shabbat or any holiday that your family celebrates.</u>

<u>What sets it apart?</u>

Allow students to give a variety of answers, most will have to do with specific things that their families do. The point is that what people do to celebrate is what sets celebrations apart from regular times.

> Now I'd like you to read "The Sabbath Taste." This is a midrashic story. The version you're going to read comes from a book written for young children, but the message of the story has to do with us.

If there are students who used the Melton curriculum in the alef year, you might want to tell them that they may recognize the story from there. After students have read the story, ask:

<u>What's the message of this story?</u>

> (That the specialness of Shabbat comes from the efforts that people make when they are actually celebrating it).

So now we have two different ideas as to the source of holiday holiness:

> the source of the holiness, that is, the specialness of these holidays, comes from God;

> the source of the holiness, that is, the specialness of these holidays comes from people.

So that it will be easier for students to focus on these two separate ideas, write them both on board:

Source of holiness—God

Source of holiness—people

<u>Which do you think is the real source of holiness, or separate specialness of a holiday?</u>

Allow time for discussion. This is an open-ended question with no one right answer.

I think it probably works both ways. The holidays that we have mentioned so far are Biblical. Their holiness in the Bible is attributed to God. But, without us doing something to mark them, to set them aside, they will become unknown. For example, if we don't set aside Pesah as a special time, if we don't attend a seder, if we don't make Pesah different from the rest of the days of the year, then it may still appear on a calendar—and there may be people who celebrate it—but for us it will have no holiness, no separateness, no set apartness.

There are holidays like Purim or Hanukkah or Yom Ha'atzma'ut, that we have talked about this year, that we know <u>people</u> have set aside as holidays. Again, if we don't mark those times, by going to synagogue and reading the Megillah or by lighting a חֲנֻכִּיָּה or saying Hallel, then for us those holidays will cease to exist as days of holiness.

Closing

As you approach your Bar/ Bat mitzvah year, this is a really important issue. Because now you become, according to Jewish tradition, adult members of the community. It's up to you what happens to these holidays in your own lives and in the lives of your future families.

I'd like to give you a list of holidays we've mentioned today. Work in pairs. Choose three holidays—and come up with a suggestion for what a person your age can do to add holiness to these days.

Worksheet is attached. As students fill it out, you might make a large version on the board. Then when students have completed their charts, you can fill in the large chart with their answers.

WORKSHEET

Holidays
What are some of the things a person your
age can do to add holiness, uniqueness to this holiday?

Answer the question in the right hand column for 3 holidays.

שַׁבָּת	
רֹאשׁ הַשָּׁנָה	
יוֹם כִּפּוּר	
רֹאשׁ חֹדֶשׁ	
פֶּסַח	
שָׁבֻעוֹת	
סֻכּוֹת	

www.ingramcontent.com/pod-product-compliance
Lightning Source LLC
Chambersburg PA
CBHW081633040426
42449CB00014B/3295